G000043633

QUESTIONING IDENTITIES;
PHILOSOPHY IN PSYCHOANALYTIC
PRACTICE

QUESTIONING IDENTITIES; PHILOSOPHY IN PSYCHOANALYTIC PRACTICE

Mary Lynne Ellis
and Noreen O'Connor

KARNAC

First published in 2010 by
Karnac Books Ltd
118 Finchley Road
London NW3 5HT

Copyright © 2010 by Mary Lynne Ellis and Noreen O'Connor

The right of Mary Lynne Ellis and Noreen O'Connor to be identified as the authors of this work has been asserted in accordance with §§ 77 and 78 of the Copyright Design and Patents Act 1988.

All rights reserved. No part of this publication may be reproduced, stored in a retrieval system, or transmitted, in any form or by any means, electronic, mechanical, photocopying, recording, or otherwise, without the prior written permission of the publisher.

British Library Cataloguing in Publication Data

A C.I.P. for this book is available from the British Library

ISBN-13: 978-1-85575-895-7

Typeset by Vikatan Publishing Solutions (P) Ltd., Chennai, India

Printed in Great Britain

www.karnacbooks.com

For Niamh and Len

CONTENTS

ACKNOWLEDGEMENTS   ix

INTRODUCTION   xi
Mary Lynne Ellis and Noreen O'Connor

CHAPTER ONE
Passionate differences   1
Noreen O'Connor

CHAPTER TWO
Who speaks? Who listens? Different voices
     and different sexualities   11
Mary Lynne Ellis

CHAPTER THREE
Is Melanie Klein the one who knows who you really are?   35
Noreen O'Connor

CHAPTER FOUR
The an-arche of psychoanalysis 47
Noreen O'Connor

CHAPTER FIVE
Shifting the ego towards a body subject 59
Mary Lynne Ellis

CHAPTER SIX
Subjects of perversion 85
Noreen O'Connor

CHAPTER SEVEN
(Dis)continuous identities and the time of the other 95
Mary Lynne Ellis

CHAPTER EIGHT
Images of sexualities; Language and embodiment
in art therapy 121
Mary Lynne Ellis

CHAPTER NINE
Homophobia is the patient 139
Mary Lynne Ellis

CHAPTER TEN
Listening differently in the face-to-face 153
Noreen O'Connor

REFERENCES 175

INDEX 183

ACKNOWLEDGEMENTS

We are very grateful to Niamh O'Connor and Leonard Kelleher for their support and for the generous contribution of their professional skills. We would also like to thank our friends and colleagues, particularly Jane Aaron, Roger Bacon, Sally Berry, Maureen Cantwell, Daphne Degotardi, Liz Lloyd, Ide ní Laoghaire, Veronica Norburn, Mercedes Nuñez, and Tom Ryan. We have been inspired and helped over the years by their thoughtfulness and their integrity. We are especially appreciative of Tina Chanter and Heather Townsend for their philosophical imagination and clarity. Thank you too to Rachel Assaf for the originality of her artistic input.

We are grateful to the publishers of the following articles and book chapters for permission to include them in this book:

O'Connor, N. (1990). The An-arche of psychotherapy. In: J. Fletcher and A. Benjamin (Eds.), *Abjection, Melancholia and Love, the Work of Julia Kristeva*, pp. 42–52. London and New York: Routledge. Reproduced by permission of Taylor and Francis Books (UK).

O'Connor, N. (1990). Is Melanie Klein the one who knows who you really are? *Women: A Cultural Review*. Vol 1:2, pp. 180–188.

Oxford: Oxford University Press. Reproduced by permission of Taylor and Francis Group, Informa UK Ltd. (http:/www. informaworld.com).

O'Connor, N. (1995). Passionate differences: lesbianism, post-modernism, and psychoanalysis. From *Disorienting Sexuality*. By T. Domenici and R.C. Lessor (Eds.). Reproduced by permission of Routledge/Taylor and Francis Group LLC.

Ellis, M.L. (1997). Who speaks? Who listens? Different voices and different sexualities. *British Journal of Psychotherapy, Volume 13*, No. 3, pp. 369–383. London: Artesian Books. Reproduced by permission of John Wiley and Sons, Chichester, UK.

O'Connor, N. (2001). Subjects of perversion. In: A. Mollino and C. Ware (Eds.), *Where Id Was*. London: Continuum, pp. 87–95. Reproduced by kind permission of Continuum International Publishing Group.

Ellis, M.L. (2007). Images of sexualities: language and embodiment in art therapy. *International Journal of Art therapy: Inscape*. Vol. 12:2, pp. 60–68. Oxon, UK: Taylor and Francis. Reproduced by permission of Taylor and Francis Group, Informa UK Ltd. (http:/www.informaworld.com).

Ellis, M.L. (2008). (Dis)continuous identities and the time of the other. In: Ellis, M.L., *Time In Practice, Analytical Perspectives on the Times of our Lives*. London: Karnac, 2008, pp. 107–131. Reproduced by kind permission of Karnac.

Ellis, M.L. (2008). Homophobia is the patient. *Sitegeist*, No. 1, Spring, 2008. London: Karnac, 2008, pp. 29–43. Reproduced by kind permission of Karnac.

INTRODUCTION

Mary Lynne Ellis and Noreen O'Connor

What can philosophy add to the wealth of theorizing in the analytic tradition? Are philosophical questions not too abstract and irrelevant to clinical practice? Has philosophical writing anything to add to psychoanalytic theorizing of the vicissitudes of normal/pathological development? Our book *Questioning Identities: Philosophy in Psychoanalytic Practice* introduces a range of contemporary European philosophical perspectives which have been influential in our clinical practices. Questions of "identity" permeate the writing of philosophers in the contemporary European tradition, such as Heidegger, Merleau-Ponty, Levinas, Foucault, and Butler. We explore the relevance to the analytical relationship of their perspectives on language, mind/body, time, history, culture, class, gender, race and sexuality. Reflection on these issues is vital for the expansion of our appreciation of the conscious and unconscious experiences and perceptions of identities and intersubjectivities. Questions regarding the status of claims of "normal/abnormal" and "natural/unnatural" are intrinsic to such themes. We show how attention to these perspectives allows for more nuanced, subtle, and complex ways of listening/responding and of articulating that which has, from the beginning, been at the heart of psychoanalysis, namely case presentations of the relationship between the analyst and the patient.

Our book is a crucial intervention at a critical point in the history of psychoanalysis. Arguments for and against statutory regulation of psychotherapists pertain to the status of the kinds of knowledge claimed by practitioners, the kinds of techniques which follow from it, the kinds of ethical judgements which regulate it, and the kind of political society which these ethical values express. All of these questions contain explicit or implicit assumptions about subjectivity, about how we know "who" or what is reality, truth, existence, love, suffering, happiness, and justice.

Philosophers' influence on psychoanalysts, as Ellis (2008) indicates in her book, *Time In Practice*, is not always acknowledged, yet it can be discerned in the work of Freud, Jung, Winnicott, Fanon, Lacan, and Laing. Freud was for a period a student of Brentano's, the German philosopher who taught Husserl; Lacan; Merleau-Ponty were engaged in public debate in France. In Jung's work there are many references to philosophers, particularly Schopenhauer, Nieztsche, Spinoza and Leibnitz. Contemporaneously Jessica Benjamin (1990), through her reading of Hegal and Habermas, develops a theory of intersubjectivity and gender which crucially challenges dualisms of subject/object and emphasizes the importance of recognition of others' differences.

20th and 21st centrury contemporary European philosophers and queer, gender, women's studies and post-colonial theorists variously debate how, and to what extent, psychoanalytic and/or post-modernist theorizing account for the constructions of lesbian, gay, queer, bisexual, heterosexual, and trans-gendered subjectivities and identities within specific class and cultural contexts. For example, Ahmed (2006), in her book *Queer Phenomenology*, presents critically queer readings of Freud and Fanon in her original phenomenological analysis of orientation and embodiment in relation to gender, race, and sexuality. Writers in these fields have increasingly expressed interest in the contributions of psychoanalytic practitioners who engage daily with the complexities, conflicts, confusions, and pleasures which shape the lived desires and identities of individuals who consult them. The crucial importance of a cross-disciplinary "dialogue between psychoanalysts and philosophers, feminists, gay men, people who by virtue of their place in society question established norms and practices" (see Noreen O'Connor, p. 44) is emphasized throughout our book.

We are both trained and practising psychoanalytically and we teach contemporary European philosophy. Most of the chapters in this book have been presented as lectures and published as individual articles in books and journals on psychoanalysis and contemporary European philosophy. Although over the past two decades there have been significant changes in the law and in the positions of many individual psychoanalytic practitioners with regard to sexual orientation, many schools of psychoanalysis and psychoanalytic psychotherapy, counselling, and arts therapies continue to rely on uncritical readings of traditional psychoanalytic texts for explanations of the development of sexual and gender identities. Such texts rarely address questions of race and class and tend to share the view that the attainment of heterosexuality is integral to a successful analysis. It is claimed that the "causes" of homosexuality which require analysis include, for example, fixation at an early stage of infantile or child development, problematic identifications at the Oedipal stage, fears of envious and destructive feelings and desires for reparation (related to the schizoid and depressive positions respectively), and defences against fragmentation and psychosis. A recent survey (Bartlett et al., 2009) indicates that 17 per cent of psychotherapists in Britain have assisted patients in the reduction of lesbian and gay feelings.

It is only relatively recently, in the 1990s, that such perspectives began to be subjected to serious critique by a small number of psychoanalytic psychotherapists who identified as lesbian, gay, bisexual or feminist. The first book to appear in Britain which raised these issues was *Wild Desires and Mistaken Identities, Lesbianism and Psychoanalysis*, co-authored by Noreen O'Connor and Joanna Ryan. Its challenging analysis of how lesbian sexuality is theorized by Freud, Klein, Jung, Lacan, Deutsch and their contemporary followers highlights how "homosexuality has been the site of some of the worst excesses of psychoanalysis—gross and inadequate generalizations, explicitly manipulative goals of therapy ..." (O'Connor & Ryan, 1993, p. 14). Arguing against the pathologisation of lesbianism and the universality of the Oedipus complex in psychoanalytic theorizing Noreen O'Connor and Joanna Ryan draw on contemporary European philosophical thinking to initiate a theorizing of lesbian identities which takes into account their socio-historical and cultural specificity and the uniqueness of individuals' desires. They argue for an openness in psychoanalytic theory which "can encompass the theoretical changes that are required by new and different possibilities" (1993, p. 271). *Questioning Identities: Philosophy in Psychoanalytic Practice* develops these themes in relation to a range of identities.

We are respectful and appreciative of the analytic traditions which offer original and nuanced phenomenologies of psychic pain and suffering in their relational complexities and value many of their basic tenets: their recognition of the limits of rationality in human subjectivity, their engagement with those aspects of our experience of which we are unconscious, their acknowledgement of the significance of our histories and of the transferential relationship. However, in recognizing these we are not thereby tacitly denying the myriad questions regarding their foundational claims to know what is normal human relational development. These claims for "objectivity" of knowledge are frequently conflated with moral judgements based on the evidence of clinical outcomes. This is problematic when the theories which the practices articulate are not themselves open to question within their own frames of reference. This book arises from our conviction based on our experiences that each human being is far more complex than can be encompassed by any one psychoanalytic framework. This conviction is a central tenet of postmodernist psychoanalytic practices.

A crucial feature of the book is our inclusion of clinical material, which illustrates how our perspective informs our analytical practices. In order to preserve the confidentiality of our patients we present composite examples. After much reflection we have decided to describe the identities of the individuals we see in analysis as "patients" in order to stress the patience required for analytic work. This contrasts with the term "client" which can imply, within a consumerist discourse, the acquisition of an already created product. Our aim is not to argue that our experience with our patients provides "proof" of the validity of our positions, as for example, Freud, Klein, and Jung often claim. We also do not assume that the conscious and unconscious connections made by our patients are causally determinate of the difficulties they bring to their analysis. The clinical material attests to the engagement between/of patient/analyst as generative of new ways of speaking of oneself as in Wittgensteinian terms, where new language is a new form of life.

We have found that individuals who describe themselves as suffering from discrimination because of their expressed identities do so as a result of exclusionary practices rather than because of an intrinsic psychopathology. Shared struggles against oppression constitute a socio-political identity and this does not signify a pathology. As Samuels acknowledges in his book, *the Political Psyche*, "(i)n late modernity there is scarcely the possibility of subjectivity divorced from a sense of marginality, woundedness and an accompanying grief—that is, subjection" (Samuels, 1993, p. 37). Our theorizing of identities does not in any way preclude an acknowledgement of the importance of identities empowering for individuals and groups. The ambiguity in the title of our book, *Questioning Identities: Philosophy in Psychoanalytic Practice* includes the notion of identities as challenging discrimination and/or dominant discourses.

The work of Chanter, a contemporary philosopher, is pertinent to our interpretations of the different ways in which our patients speak in identificatory terms about themselves. She argues that

> categories of identity based on the signifiers of race, gender, class, or sexuality are far from self-evident. Not only does any knowledge claimed on the basis of identifying with such categories have to be achieved as the product of critical self-reflection, the categories themselves are historically and politically implicated in one another in ways that render them contestable (Chanter, 2008, p. 28).

Our clinical material exemplifies our emphasis on interpretations of identities as inter-related and shifting according to individuals' possibilities of voicing their experiences, conscious and unconscious, of particular historical and cultural contexts. Implicit in our position is a critique of any notion of identity which presupposes it as a delineated psychic state already identified by someone else to be achieved or established. Therefore, throughout our book we emphasise the critical importance of the emergence in analysis of an original *poeisis* of the patient's own language, the articulation verbally and non-verbally of the dynamism of their lived relationships in the world. This is in contrast to self-descriptions which are either static or objectifying. Self-descriptions of this type may also be presented as identifications with particular diagnoses such as depression, alcoholism, anorexia, compulsive eating, drug addiction, and phobias etc. As Butler argues in her chapter "Critically Queer" (in *Bodies that Matter*),

> the impossibility of ... ever fully inhabiting the name by which one's social identity is inaugurated and mobilized, implies the instability and incompleteness of subject-formation. The "I" is thus a citation of the place of the "I" in speech, where that place has a certain priority and anonymity with respect to the life it animates ... (Butler, 1993, p. 226).

In her book *Gender Trouble* Butler points out that "theories of identity which elaborate predicates of colour, sexuality, ethnicity, class, and ablebodiedness invariably close with an ... etc. at the end of the list" (Butler, 1990, p. 143). She argues that the *et cetera* points to the illimitable excess of the process of signification itself in that no exhaustive list of adjectives can encompass the "subject". As Kearney writes in *The Wake of Imagination*, "... narrative identity is a *task* of imagination, not a *fait accompli*" (1994, p. 396). This task is threaded through narratives of poetry, ethics, and politics.

Our interest in language is reflected in our appreciation of biography and literature in interpretations of identities in psychoanalytic work. The black feminist writer Lorde's vivid and poetic novel *Zami* offers original insights into the complexities of lived identities as black and lesbian within the racist and homophobic culture of 1950s America. Thomas Mann's *Magic Mountain* poignantly explores the alienating effects of imposition of the time and routines of a sanatorium on the identities of its patients. Through her moving descriptions of how she negotiates of her shifting identities as a young Jewish immigrant who leaves Poland for Canada and later moves to America Hoffman highlights the significance of time, language, and embodiment through these transitions. Through their central characters all of these authors offer reflections which elucidate how desires and identities are lived and articulated and which are highly relevant to analytical practices.

Questioning Identities: Philosophy in Psychoanalytic Practice opens with examples of quotations from patients voicing agonising experiences for which they may seek help from an analyst. In Chapter One, "Passionate differences", O'Connor explores, through her comparison of modernist and post-modernist analytical approaches, the significance of the often unacknowledged philosophical assumptions and value-judgments which subtend the analyst's interpretations of patients' speech in the analytical relationship. Through her reading of Foucault, Butler, and Grosz, she challenges the mind/body dualisms pervasive in psychoanalytic writing. O'Connor presents a case-study of a young white woman, Jenny, who is torn by her conflictual feelings regarding sexual relations with men and women. Her account emphasizes the importance of the analysts' openness to the specificity of the language of the erotic transference and Jenny's unconscious experiences of her sexuality without adhering to rigid notions of sexual identity as either heterosexual or lesbian.

In Chapter Two, "Who speaks? Who listens? Different voices and different sexualities", Ellis discusses the relevance to psychoanalytic practices of Foucault's analysis of sexuality as discursive and his challenge to interpretations of sexual identities which presuppose a split between identity as "psychic", sociohistorical, and cultural. Ellis reflects on the contribution of Audre Lorde's analyses of identities and differences in her novel Zami, which explores intimate experiences between black women in the social context of 1950s McCarthyite America. Through two extensive case studies Ellis highlights the relevance of Foucault's and Lorde's theorising to clinical practice: Gloria is a mixed race lesbian who is driven in her search for an identity by an overwhelming terror of annihilation and Derek is a white middle-class Catholic man, who is married to a woman and guiltily engages in gay relationships. Ellis emphasizes the ways in which sexual identities are intertwined with those of gender, race, class, and religion and explores how Gloria and Derek's unconscious anxieties in relation to these themes emerged in their transferences to her. She also raises the question as to what informs our designation of psychopathology to certain sexual practices such as "water-sports" which are consensual and experienced as mutually pleasurable.

In the third chapter "Is Melanie Klein the one who knows who you really are?" O'Connor discusses the normative and foundationalist character of Klein's theorizing of gender and sexuality. While acknowledging Klein's contribution to interpretations of psychosis and her concomitant challenge to the primacy of pharmacological treatments, O'Connor presents a critical analysis of Klein's reliance on biologistic arguments to support Klein's claim that the attainment of heterosexuality is a central criterion for the termination of a successful analysis. She points out that Klein and her followers such as Segal ignore twentieth century advances in philosophical theorizing which problematize dualisms of "internal" and "external", thought and language. O'Connor highlights how Klein's theorizing relies on a set of a prior assumptions which are presented as "facts" or "knowledge" about the human psyche; this exemplifies the Western ideal of "self-possession" and does not allow for differences and for competing theories. Klein's and post-Kleinians' (such as Meltzer's) theorizing of lesbian sexuality as pathological per se denies the value-judgements which are inherent in their claims. For lesbians seeking psychoanalysis (and others) this matters in practice because of its a priori reification of desires.

The question of a theorizing and practice, which allows for the multiplicity of interpretations of identities is explored in Chapter Four, "The an-arche of psychoanalysis", through O'Connor's discussion of the possibilities and limitations of Kristeva's work. Plato's invocation of the Stranger in *Phaedo* is highlighted as relevant to analytic work. O'Connor reflects on the potential of Kristeva's view that the patient is "dazed" by the unexpectedness of the analyst's interpretations and that his/her desire for the Other sustains the analysis. This unexpectedness arises from the analyst's refusal to speak from within an already established foundational system or prescriptive morality. Examples of Kristeva's concern with the specificity of states of suffering are revealed in her interpretations of borderline psychosis, phobias and narcissism. Her position is, however, compromised by her claims that homosexuality is associated with narcissism and that lesbianism has its source in lack of separation from the mother. O'Connor introduces Levinas's notion of the "face-to-face", the relationship to "the Other" through which Levinas affirms the uniqueness of each human being, challenging claims to know the Other and efforts to categorize them. She highlights the relevance of this for analytical practices which are open to the uniqueness of patients' experiences and identities.

In the fifth chapter, "Shifting the ego towards a body subject" Ellis focuses on Freud's later formulations of the ego in *The Ego and the Id* (1923) and how these are related to culturally specific notions of what is "healthy" or "mature". Ellis identifies the ways in which Freud's theorizing of the ego is influenced by Enlightenment thinkers and their conviction that science gives us access to true and certain knowledge of the world. By contrast, Ellis argues, post-colonial writers and contemporary European philosophers (Walton, Heidegger, Merleau-Ponty, Foucault, Grosz and Butler) variously emphasize the significance of language, power, history, and culture in the formation of the gendered subject. In her case example of a young working-class, mixed race lesbian, Ellis describes how Elaine's difficulty in accepting the fluidity of her subjectivity may be viewed as analogous to Freud's theorizing of the ego as universal and heterosexual. Through the analytical relationship, to which Ellis brings a phenomenological perspective, Elaine begins to explore more playful and fluid experiences of her identities in their ambiguity.

O'Connor in Chapter Six, "Subjects of perversion", addresses the concept of perversion and the questions it generates regarding the conceptualisation of subjectivity in analytical practices. Through her discussion of her work with Nigel, a white Welsh man, O'Connor considers the limitations of Freud's theory of fetishism. Nigel's secret is that what gives him the excitement necessary to ejaculate is the tying of a piece of blue satin ribbon around his penis. O'Connor questions the universality of Freud's interpretation of the fetish as disavowal. For Nigel the blue ribbon emerges as being crucial to Nigel, not as a "missing penis" but specifically as one of the few things in his life that he knows to be his very own. O'Connor elucidates the way in which Nigel's desire to feel comfortable in the world is associated with his desire to know the "truth" of his identity. Arguing against Whitebook's modernist interpretations of Freud and his characterization of post-modernism as an identification with the irrational, the transgressive, and a denial of trauma she demonstrates how a modernist perspective, aimed at strengthening Nigel's ego, would have replicated the belief system which was already suffocating him.

In Chapter Seven, "(Dis)continuous identities and the time of the other", Ellis explores the relation between time and identity. Beginning with Mann's account through the characters in his novel, *The Magic Mountain*, of time as "lived" (contrasted with time as chronological), Ellis explores different philosophical conceptions of the subject's relation to time, including, through Heidegger, their death in the future. She contrasts Merleau-Ponty's view of the subject as having a continuous identity through time with Foucault's who emphasizes the gaps and ruptures which occur in history. Ellis critically reflects on differing conceptualizations within psychoanalytic theorising of the relation between psychic health and experiences of continuity and discontinuity in individuals' identities. This question is further elucidated by Ellis in the case vignette of her work with Owen who is troubled by experiences of being moved into a time which is unreachable by others and which, he says, differ from creative states of absorption. In the final part of the chapter Ellis discusses the contribution of Levinas's theorizing to conceptualising how change occurs in the analytical relationship.

Ellis, in Chapter Eight, "Images of sexualities: language and embodiment in art therapy" interweaves her reflections on language, embodiment, and identities from a phenomenological perspective with descriptions of her work with women in a workshop entitled "Am I a Lesbian?" Ellis describes how the use of imagery offered the women, who hoped to find certainty about their identities as lesbian or heterosexual, a language for their embodiment in its ambiguity and complexity. She contrasts Kahn's reductionistic interpretations of lesbian sexuality with the poetry of the women's own articulations (visual, tactile and verbal). Their imagery is illustrative of Merleau-Ponty's claim that the expression in dreams, pictures, literature and music is indistinguishable from what is expressed: for example, for Sandra her perception of orgasm with a woman at that moment was a field of red poppies. The specificity of this, as Merleau-Ponty argues, is obliterated by recourse to notions of the unconscious as a discreet world of impulses completely distinct from consciousness, and also of body and mind as separate entities. The question as to how the political contingency of identities can also include recognition of individual differences (addressed by Lorde's writing) featured centrally in the group.

Ellis highlights the contribution of Fanon's theorizing of the effects of racism on black people's identities and Foucault's analysis of the discursive production of sexualities to her responses to Sandra who was facing the possibility of being doubly stigmatised as black and lesbian.

In Chapter Nine, "Homophobia is the patient" Ellis shifts the focus from the effects of homophobia on lesbian, gay, and bisexual patients to a consideration of the phenomenon of homophobia. Such an intervention becomes increasingly urgent in a context where significant changes in the law have not sufficiently altered homophobic attitudes. Ellis's aim is not to offer a definitive explanation of homophobia(s) but, rather, to introduce a number of possible, not necessarily mutually exclusive interpretations of it. Through a discussion of work with a patient, Tesesa, who is distraught at her son's revelation that he identifies as gay, Ellis considers the untenability of Freud's theorizing of phobias and the limitations of Young-Bruehl's categorization of homophobic character types to account for Teresa's anxieties. She reflects on the various discourses which shape Teresa's responses to her son including her Catholicism (Teresa is from a working-class Italian background) and her assumption, derived from popular psychoanalytic thought, that she had "caused" her son's homosexuality. These were intertwined with feelings of loss and terrors of the "unknown". Ellis discusses the relevance of Butler's theorizing of the melancholia which arises from the inability to mourn the lost (prohibited) object of homosexual desire. Levinas's notion of the Other as unknown highlights the extent to which Teresa's homophobia may also have been an attempt to absorb her son into "the same", unable to allow him to escape her power.

In "Listening differently in the face-to-face", Chapter Ten, O'Connor expands on the clinical relevance of Levinas's theorizing to clinical practices. She traces some of Levinas's questions regarding the emergence of a sense of self in lived states of anxieties, in the unrelenting weightiness of insomnia, in laziness, in the fatigue of indolence (conceptualised in psychoanalytic texts as depression). His detailed phenomenological descriptions of these experiences contribute to the originality of O'Connor's interpretations of the specificity of the suffering of her patient, Kieran. A middle-class Irish young man married with children, Kieran is weighted by lethargy and feelings of pointlessness. His crisis revolves around his refusal of the particular identity expected of him as a man by his business family and his terror of his own individuality. O'Connor explores how, through Kieran's speaking with her in the "face-to-face" a new position in relation to his past emerges for him. She emphasizes that this is not a matter of tracing past intricacies which are already drawn to bring these to conscious rational appropriation but, rather, a lived acknowledgement of a call to respond to this otherness which is intrinsic to each of our own selves in the face-to-face relationship.

CHAPTER ONE

Passionate differences

Noreen O'Connor

"I am feeling numb, dragging through the grey days, it's all worthless".

"The pain is killing me, there is no let up".

"I'm so lonely I could die".

"People scare me—I know when women see me they want to murder me".

"The only relief is the sight of blood".

"I can't stop, only the chocolate and cakes give me comfort, I hide my fat body from the world".

"Masturbation is agony, it leaves my body in pain for days".

"John hates me".

"Jane abused me".

As analysts we listen to examples of suffering daily, attending to the nuances of past and present relationships. Are we listening for the clues to the repressed libido, the part-object relation of the paranoid schizoid position, or the repetition of the unconscious drives destabilizing the fiction of a unified ego?

Do these questions matter? In other words, how does our theory and training as analysts influence our practices? Would you, on

1

hearing someone in emotional pain, advise that person to go and see a post-modernist; or a modernist for that matter? Modernism and post-modernism are terms which express differing Western cultural ethoses. Each is characterized by its position on history, truth, power, morality, the human subject, masculinity, and femininity. It is not that there is just one exclusive theory of modernism or post-modernism—different writers construct specific conceptual frameworks, which elaborate their understanding of the modern or the post-modern.

Modernism refers to a view of the subject as rational, having a stable identity, which can be universally known. The subject is construed in terms of an essential representation. History is seen to be linear, teleological. Power is ascribed to the "one who knows" and who therefore has the right to legislate for the truth and value of others. Post-modernism, on the other hand, stresses the de-centering of rationality in subjectivity, the multiplicity of shifting identifications, the interweaving of language and subjectivity. In other words, emphasis is placed on psychic development as inextricably bound up with linguistic and social development. Consequently, post-modernists argue that subjectivity is not adequately theorized in terms of universal developmental mechanisms or stages occurring outside of a social/linguistic context. Emphasis on the linguistic/social character of subjectivity maintains shifting complexities and, through questioning fixed assumptions of the "human", allows for wider theoretical development. This is especially relevant for psychoanalytic analyses of subjectivity and to the question of whether or not psychoanalyses can move on from traditional Oedipal interpretations of masculinity, femininity, and sexual desires in order to allow the theorizing required by new relational possibilities. History in a post-modern view is characterized by gaps, losses, repetitions, and changing perspectives.

Historically, modernity has been situated as emerging with the Enlightenment, exemplarily expressed in Kant's philosophy. Kant introduced a critique of traditionally held beliefs in favour of a notion of the human as characterized by the exercise of autonomous critical reason. The humanism of modernity conceives of the human as the subject who can know himself:

The guarantee that everything that has eluded him may be
restored to him; the certainty that time will dispense nothing without restoring it in a reconstituted unity; the promise
that one day the subject ... will once again be able to appropriate ... all these things that are kept at a distance by difference
(Foucault, 1972, p. 12).

Michel Foucault, in his work on the history of sexuality, situates
Freud as a modernist because of his positioning of the Oedipus
myth as the cornerstone of psychoanalysis. Oedipus pursues the
"truth" of his "identity" hidden from consciousness yet constituted by desire and sexuality. Identification is a crucial concept
in psychoanalytic accounts of development and in the concomitant process of analysis. The assured polarities of mother-father,
feminine-masculine are the dyad of identifications and repudia-
tions attributed to the baby/child's gender and sexual identification. Moreover, it is this gender identification with its appropriate
sexual alignment that psychoanalysis privileges. In our book *Wild
Desires and Mistaken Identities, Lesbianism and Psychoanalysis*, Joanna
Ryan and I reviewed the major texts of the psychoanalytic tradition
regarding their theories of lesbianism. Within these texts we identified recurring issues:

The alignment of gender and sexuality in the notion of identification and desire; the reliance on concepts such as oral sadism
and unconscious identification with the father as developmental explanations; the consignment of homosexuality to the pre-
oedipal and the narcissistic; the appeal to biological phenomena
as constitutive of psychic reality; the *a priori* theorizing based on
normative notions of innate heterosexuality; the obliviousness
to countertransference problems stemming from the personal
and theoretical position of the practitioner (O'Connor & Ryan,
1993, pp. 12–13).

The concept of identification is construed as representation. Knowing who or what you are is knowing that you are a man or a woman
and knowing who or what you desire. Not knowing whether you
are a man or a woman is designated as "hysterical". Representation

implies knowledge, a bringing-together, a representing of the past and diversity of knowledge by means of which the subject claims to know himself completely. Foucault and his successors offer critiques of the notion of personal identity as equated with sexual identity: "our sexuality reveals us to ourselves, and our desire to have this secret self-knowledge revealed drives us to engage in discourse on our sexuality" (Bernauer & Mahon, 1994, p. 129). This is the celebrated critique of the "repressive hypothesis". Foucault argues that psychoanalysis analyzes sexuality in terms of repression and in doing so operates with a substantive notion of the "human" with the notion of a "true" underlying sexual identity.

Judith Butler offers a fascinating critique of sexuality conceived in terms of identity politics. She argues that identity categories of, for example, lesbian, homosexual, heterosexual, etc. are inadequate because every "subject position" is a matrix of different power relationships which are not univocal. In other words, subjectivity is not a matter of a self-identical entity. Butler points out that installing alternative gender identities reproduces normative exclusionary practices which foreclose the questioning of gender and sexuality. Rather, she allows for differing subject positions while challenging the notion of universal foundational humans who know themselves in their "true" sexuality. According to Butler, "The subject is not a thing ... but a process of signification within an open system of discursive possibilities" (Sawacki, 1994, p. 299).

Post-modernists challenge humanistic modernism, with its ideal of the self who knows himself and is thereby free, by focussing on the contingency and specificity of our lives. The problem is not just that psychoanalysis has got it wrong in relation to homosexuality and got it right about heterosexuality, but rather that the psychoanalytic enterprise of equating human subjectivity with the truth of sexuality is a construal of human relationships in terms of a totalizing knowledge, the refusal of difference and otherness, and a neglect of relationships as ethically recalcitrant to full knowledge. This is why postmodernism is relevant to our psychoanalytic practices; it keeps us alive to the dangers of imagining that we exhaustively know the psyche, and it keeps us alive to our responsibility to and the uniqueness of our relationships with each human being.

In classical psychoanalytic theory and practice homosexuality is considered to be non-pathological if it is surpassed, if it is seen as adolescent experimentation, as a preparation for "adult," genital sexuality. Developmental theory construed in terms of mechanistic, causal determinism, such as is the case for all the psychoanalytic writers who universalize homosexuality as pathological, precludes a questioning of its own methods and assumptions regarding truth, knowledge, and morality. Despite the rigour and sensitivity of some of their clinical material, their desire for a universal metapsychology prevents them from hearing the specificity of the patient's speech. These psychoanalytic writers begin by *a priori* pathologizing homosexuality as a unitary phenomenon and then theorize the origins of the pathology they have assumed. This has a certain logical contradiction and merits psychoanalytic interest. Psychoanalysts such as Socarides who trace homosexuality back to pre-Oedipal fixation resulting in disordered gender identity, primitive defence mechanisms, and fragile ego boundaries, consistently assert that all homosexuality is pathological and therefore consider the psychoanalytic task to be treating homosexual patients to change their sexual orientation. Here the complexities of love and hate are reduced to ascriptions of primitive eroticism involving the dyadic mother/baby.

We are indebted to post-modern analyses for pointing out that the body and its development is not a-cultural and a-historical. As I have previously argued, sexual differences are bodily differences, and sexual identity

> (p)ermeates, mediates, and is mediated by all our social and cultural interactions. Sexual identity is not simply a question of isolated individuals repressing or discovering their "true" desires, or of a logical definition, but is variously inscribed in cultural, religious, legal and political systems and practices (O'Connor & Ryan, 1993, p. 22).

Michael Foucault's work on the history of sexuality, as I have mentioned, indicates that sexual behaviour is a matter of "how the rendering of sexual behaviour into discourses comes to be transformed, what types of jurisdiction and veridiction it is subject to and how constitutive elements of this domain come to be called 'sexuality'" (Foucault, 1987, p. 116). Thus for Foucault the body does not give knowledge that is then merely transmitted by an essentially neutral language. What is categorized as normal/abnormal, natural/unnatural are social constructs arising out of power/knowledge relationships rather than factual distinctions given at the level of the body or of the individual psyche.

Elizabeth Grosz points to the traditional binary categories defining the body: "inside/outside, subject/object, active/passive, fantasy/reality, surface/depth" (Grosz, 1995, p. 196). Grosz challenges this dualistic opposition and points out that libidinal intensities are not confined to biologically determined zones but are interactions occurring on the surface of the skin and various organs. In her view, concepts of inside and outside need not be oppositional. Grosz argues that what she calls "surface effects" generate an underlying depth or consciousness just like the moebius strip, a continuous two-dimensional plane which when rotated in space creates an inside and an outside:

> Tracing the outside of the moebius strip leads one directly to
> its inside without at any point leaving the surface. This depth
> is one of the distinguishing features marking out the modern
> Western capitalist body from other kinds (Grosz, 1995, p. 198).

In line with a post-modern perspective, I am strategically challenging a dualistic account of the body/psyche, which is pervasive in psychoanalytic writing; that is, the claim to know that there are discreet inner and outer worlds, and that the developmental task is to link them by virtue of theories of phantasies and mechanisms of defences and repressions. This is not to deny the importance of theories of development but it is to stress that arguments in terms of causal mechanisms are inadequate to the rich complexity of human bodily/linguistic development, to the development of the child in its relationship to others (see Merleau-Ponty, 1964a, pp. 96–155). Neither am I discounting the crucial importance of the baby's early experiences prior to the acquisition of syntactical language.

From the beginning, the baby is in a relational, linguistic world, albeit pre-verbal, which influences the vicissitudes of adult relationship but not as causally mechanical. Psychoanalysts whose conception of the baby's earliest relationship as that to phantasized objects where the phantasies are postulated as being a-linguistic, not just pre-verbal, advocate baby-observation as crucial to learning about early developmental stages. Apart from the epistemological naïveté regarding "observation," such theorists could be accused of falling into the same mistake as did early social researchers like anthropologists, who mistakenly believe that they could "objectively" analyze cultures without attending to the significance of their own investigative presence for their results. It is important to emphasize that homosexuality and heterosexuality are not adequately theorized within a normative mechanical discourse—living lovers and haters are culturally specific in their self-understandings, their passions, and their mortalities.

In offering a critical appraisal of development construed in terms of causal mechanisms, I am not in any way discounting the pain, loss, terror, abandonment, abuse, and rejection that can plunge a young person into pathological, destructive relationships in the world. The question is whether psychoanalysts can acknowledge, theoretically and in practice, that a young person's homosexual orientation can lead progressively to mature adult relationships as a homosexual, or if it is necessarily regressive in adulthood.

The purpose of psychoanalytic case studies is to illustrate common features and specific diversity and complexity. The "common features" within the clinical setting are traditionally rendered as indices of the pathological, which is open to "scientific" or at the least hermeneutical—that is, interpretive—regularization. Common features do arise in clinical work with people who are homosexual—often arising from the difficulties and strengths they struggle with in homophobic societies in which their choice of sexual partner is ridiculed, denied, or legally punishable. As Joanna Ryan and I emphasize in Wild Desires and Mistaken Identities, "if generalization is appropriate it is in the area of the structuring of lesbian oppression, rather than in anything supposedly inherent in lesbians" (O'Connor & Ryan, 1993, p. 22).

In the following case material, adolescence is seen in light of the complexities of time and subjectivity elucidated by post-modern critiques rather than in terms of a monolithic teleological explanation of development.

Jenny distraughtly stated at her first session: "I don't know who I am, I'm two people and I feel I'm going mad," and proceeded to sob deeply. She was engaged to be married to a young man whom she said she loved very much but in planning her marriage had drawn closer and closer to a friend, a young married woman, who was to be her bridesmaid. The two women were affectionate with one another and Jenny found herself "daydreaming" about Claire and feeling a sexual longing to be with her. She was confused because she had a passionate sexual relationship with her fiancé. Jenny was twenty-five, the eldest of three children—a brother and sister—and from a Northern working-class Catholic family. She had been successful and popular at school and in college and was looking forward to having her own home with John and setting up a family. Jenny quickly formed a positive transference to me and said she felt "waves washing through her" of relief that she could even speak about her feelings for Claire. She had professed to have a wonderfully close family, a mother with whom she could discuss her boyfriends and a father with whom she discussed politics. She was brought up a Catholic and her criticisms of the Church were the only points of dissension with her parents. Gradually, Jenny began to have erotic feelings for me which she reluctantly spoke of; she thought that it would mean the end of her analysis and that I would find her so disgusting that I would be instantly rejecting and angry. In holding this erotic transference, I opened the space for Jenny to explore her earlier adolescent fantasies and a passionate sexual relationship with another girl at the age of fourteen.

Jenny and her friend, Rose, were part of a group of peers that "hung around together" at school and went to discos on Saturday nights. They dated boys and discussed relative merits of "dry kisses" and "wet kisses." Members of their clique often stayed in each other's houses, and Jenny and Rose frequently shared a bed in which they discussed their religious beliefs, the boys they fancied, school, and the freedom of the future until late at night. One night "for a laugh," Rose started kissing Jenny on the mouth. Jenny experienced an overwhelmingly new bodily/sexual arousal. For the first time each of them declared passionate love for the other and swore that if the other were a boy they would get married and live together forever. The next morning Jenny found her pyjamas "wet with white stuff" and was terror stricken, convinced she had turned into boy—she had recently learned that boys had "wet dreams". She was too scared to mention it to anyone and felt it was a Divine retribution for being sexual with Rose.

Jenny's passionate lovemaking with Rose continued for two years during which time the girls continued to go out with boys.

They worried about the sinful aspect of their relationship but concluded that it "couldn't be all that serious because it wasn't sex with boys". Jenny had heard about lesbians, women who dressed in suits like men, and she certainly did not want anything to do with them. She worried that Rose was getting more and more interested in boys and began to spend evenings of agony as Rose went out with Michael. Finally, Rose told her that she was in love with him but that Jenny would always be her best friend. Jenny described agonies of loss, desolation, and deception as she tried to pretend to family friends, and school that all was well with her. She began to furtively look up medical textbooks to see if they would tell her what was wrong with her; she hated herself and felt evil and dirty for desiring Rose. Jenny enjoyed her school life and began to go out with lots of boys in the hope of finding what Rose had found with Michael and of putting her secret behind her. She began to enjoy boys sexually and met John with whom she fell in love. She felt she had at last outgrown her desire for Rose. As this history unfolded, Jenny began having negative dreams about me; I appeared as threatening, leading her to the edge of cliffs, and under the sea, and into houses with uncertain floors. The conflict between her love for John and her sense of herself and her future, and her longing for Claire, resulted in negative attacks on me for not curing her of her lesbian feelings and for even allowing her to have explicit thoughts about an amorous future with Claire. Such a future seemed impossible; she would lose her family, her friends, her job (she was a teacher); she would be destitute and shunned; and John's life would be ruined.

Jenny's conflicting feelings in relation to sexual relations with men and women were a recurrent theme in her analysis for over two years. She married John but five months later had a brief affair with a lesbian colleague with whom she was able to share her growing confidence in her intellectual interests. This relationship, whilst terrifying in its intensity, seemed to open out for her the possibility of a mutually fulfilling adult lesbian relationship. After eighteen months she decided to leave John and began a serious relationship with another woman.

This vignette illustrates how I was able to hold open the possibility of Jenny's shifting desires without adhering to a notion of a fixed sexual identity as either "really heterosexual" (and therefore "normal"/mature) or "really lesbian". Although it was challenging for me initially, I also managed to be sufficiently open to the vicissitudes of Jenny's eroticised transference, an openness which, from our experience of supervising analysts (including feminist therapists), we have found to be rare. Rather than pathologize her lesbianism, I enabled Jenny to explore her fear of sexual intensity with women. The psychoanalytic frame allowed for the working through of her merged intensity with her mother such that she could separate from her and, albeit painfully, forge a fresh relationship with her. This enabled Jenny to begin to discover an intimacy with another woman that allowed for difference and separateness. Jenny, like many psychoanalytic writers, had equated lesbianism with symbiosis and much of her analysis was concerned with her moving from such a "fixated" certainty.

For many psychoanalysts homosexuality is viewed primarily as a denial of difference, as narcissistic. Sameness of gender is assumed to be a barrier to "real" sexual desire. Such a position assumes that all features of a homosexual relationship pale into insignificance compared to the sameness of gender, including all other possibly important differences between the partners. In our experience it cannot be assumed that just because two people are of the same gender, they therefore experience gender in similar ways. In practice, many of the excitements, conflicts, and pleasure of homosexual relationships may well concern differences in the way gender is experienced and lived out, including how, as a woman, desire for and from another woman is felt and expressed. In this way, gender can be an issue of difference between two people of the same gender, either constructively or destructively, consciously or unconsciously, depending on the relationship in question.

As Joanna Ryan and I stress in *Wild Desires and Mistaken Identities*:

> A consideration ... of how psychoanalysis has thought about and dealt with homosexuality also offers many insights into perennial questions about psychoanalysis, such as the split-off nature of the social, the regressive use of the biological and the causal, the unreflective incorporation of social norms into notions of maturity, the difficulty of really letting the patient speak, and engaging with this, and finally, the complexities of rendering social forms of oppression psychoanalytically (O'Connor & Ryan, 1993, p. 13).

CHAPTER TWO

Who speaks? Who listens? Different voices and different sexualities

Mary Lynne Ellis

In this chapter I want to consider how as analysts we can respond sensitively to questions of sexuality and sexual identity that are raised for us by our patients. Psychoanalytic theories of homosexuality have been restricted to interpretations regarding the internal world where, for example, pre-Oedipal fixations or Oedipal conflicts are regarded as the "cause" of homosexuality. Such interpretations arise from a view of the truth of the individual's world (the unconscious) as being located outside or beyond the wider social context. The individual subject of psychoanalysis is ahistorical and acultural. In excluding a recognition of cultural constructions of sexuality psychoanalytic theorizing contradicts itself: in claiming that sexual identity is only partial and fragmentary it nevertheless holds to a normative view of sexuality in which heterosexual identity is equated with maturity. Even though it is claimed that heterosexuality must itself be subject to analysis (in the same way as homosexuality), a secure heterosexual identity is still, paradoxically, what is required if the analysis is to be successful.

Noreen O'Connor and Joanna Ryan, in *Wild Desires and Mistaken Identities, Lesbianism and Psychoanalysis* (1993), challenge the extensive claims within psychoanalytic theorizing that lesbianism is, for example, a symptom of arrested sexual development, a narcissistic condition, a defence against separation anxiety, psychosis or the dread of mutilation and disintegration. Central to their work is a critique of the notion of the Oedipus complex as being universal, emphasizing instead the cultural specificity of sexual identity. They highlight the crucial importance of drawing from other disciplines outside psychoanalysis to enable us to address the complexities of sexualities and notions of identity, and to be more open to the individual and constantly shifting meanings that sex and sexuality hold for our patients. They show how the writings of Foucault, Merleau-Ponty, Derrida, Butler and others in the post-modern tradition can contribute to our developing a psychoanalytic practice that is truly concerned with the speech of our patients, with complexities of transference and the uniqueness of every psychoanalytic encounter.

Noreen O'Connor and Joanna Ryan's work is informed by their recognition that questions of sexual identity have a historical relativity. However, they acknowledge that:

> An understanding of the interconnections between what is expressed psychoanalytically and what is expressed socially, in legislation and in other practices or attitudes, would require an extensive study in its own right (O'Connor & J. Ryan, 1993, p. 25).

The question of the connection between the intra-psychic and the wider social and political context has, in the past twenty-five to thirty years, increasingly preoccupied analysts. It is striking that, in Britain, the work of the philosopher Michel Foucault, has, with the exception of O'Connor and Ryan's book, been largely excluded from debates in this area. The reason may lie in the tendency of analysts in Britain to assume an already existing division between the psychic and the socio-political. Foucault claims, in contrast, that this division has itself arisen out of particular discourses that are socially and culturally specific.

In this chapter I will begin by drawing on Foucault's analysis to highlight the socio-historical specificity of lesbian and gay identities. I will show how these identities have been constituted out of complex webs of ecclesiastical, moral, legal, political and economic discourses and practices that are constantly shifting. Secondly, I will discuss aspects of Audre Lorde's (1982) novel *Zami*, and show how this offers some particularly valuable insights into the question of identity in relation to both race and sexuality and the diversity of lesbian experiences. Lastly, I will reflect on the relevance of these considerations to psychoanalytic theorizing and practice. As illustrations I will present two case studies, one of a black lesbian and one of a white, male, married patient. My aim in these case studies is to show how a Foucauldian approach can be combined with a psychoanalytic approach to enable a more sensitive understanding of issues regarding identity and sexual orientation as well as race.

In *The History of Sexuality* (1978) Foucault's central claim is that the body cannot be seen purely as a material or biological "fact". It does not exist outside discourse; what is designated as normal or abnormal, natural or unnatural, depends on the power of institutions such as the church, medicine or law, that is bought to bear on the body. His position challenges Freud's claim that the repression of sexuality has underpinned the development of bourgeois culture. Foucault argues that sexuality itself is constructed through various mechanisms and regimes of power ("polymorphous techniques of power") that permeate discourses on sexuality and both control and incite sexual pleasure (Foucault, 1978, p. 11). He claims, for example, that the meticulous surveillance of sexual practices within the bourgeois family in the nineteenth century paradoxically:

> ... acted by multiplication of singular sexualities. It did not set boundaries for sexuality; it extended the various forms of sexuality, pursuing them according to lines of indefinite penetration ... It did not set up a barrier; it provided places of maximum saturation. It produced and determined the sexual mosaic (Foucault, 1978, p. 47).

Foucault identifies the eighteenth century as marking the beginning of a multiplication of discourses on sex. Within Christianity, the confession and self-examination, particularly in relation to sexuality, increased in importance. Every thought, desire, fantasy and action had to be meticulously observed and confessed. The focus of eighteenth-century ecclesiastical laws and rules governing sexual practices concerned matrimonial relations. Sexual activities that took place outside marriage, such as adultery, rape, sodomy and incest, were regarded as extreme infringements of the law but it was only later that these came under scrutiny.

Gradually, according to Foucault, as heterosexual monogamy became increasingly established with its strictly regularized sexuality, attention shifted towards the sexuality of children, of so-called mad men and women, criminals, and those engaged in same-sex relationships. These people, previously hardly noticed, were called upon to confess what they were. They were viewed as belonging to an almost separate dimension, that of "unnatural sexuality". Jeffrey Weeks (1979, p. 27, 89) suggests that this focus on so-called sexual aberration and the search for its origins within the individual was influenced by the impact of Darwinism and the claim that survival depended on sexual selection—the ultimate test of biological success lying in reproduction.

It was within this context, as Foucault points out, that Kraft-Ebbing's (1886) *Psychopathia Sexualis*, the compendium of case studies of perversions, was published. Kraft-Ebbing was explicit in his moral judgements, condemning sexual practices other than heterosexual intercourse as being morally degenerate whilst, at the same time, viewing them as symptoms of illness. He regarded homosexuality as both acquired (particularly associated with masturbation) and congenital. His book was followed by numerous other publications that attempted detailed classifications of sexual pathologies (see Ellenberger, 1970, pp. 291–303).

Foucault (1978) cites Westphal's (1870) article on "contrary sexual sensations" as constituting the birth of the medical category of homosexuality. This article contained the origins of the notion that gender identity and sexual identity are necessarily linked through the naturalness of heterosexual object choice. For the first time the homosexual became:

> a personage, a past, a case history, and a childhood … Nothing that went into his total composition was unaffected by his sexuality. It was everywhere present in him: at the root of all his actions because it was their insidious and indefinitely active principle … (Foucault, 1978, p. 43).

The continuing debates as to whether homosexuality was innate or acquired had important consequences regarding legal penalties; it was claimed that, if it was acquired, homosexual behaviour should be deemed a criminal offence. This view was becoming increasingly prevalent and psychotherapeutic treatment was advocated as a method of treating homosexuality. It was from within this context that psychoanalytic theory developed. In *Three Essays on Sexuality*, published in 1905, Freud makes many references to Kraft-Ebbing (amongst others) as important sources for some of his theorizing.

Many of the significant developments in feminist, gender, and lesbian and gay studies have been influenced by Foucault's theorizing, emphasizing the socio-cultural and historical specificity of sexual identity and sexual practices. In their article, "On 'Compulsory heterosexuality and lesbian existence': defining the issues", Ferguson et al. (1982) argue that the possibilities for lesbianism emerged as a consequence of women's economic independence from men. The growth of urban areas enabled women to leave the confines of small patriarchal farming communities and to free themselves increasingly from their emotional and sexual dependence on men. In her paper, "Identity crises: Who is a lesbian anyway?", the sociologist Vera Whisman (1993) offers a succinct and thoughtful history of lesbian identity—from the "true invert", the masculine lesbian, Stephen Gordon from Radcliffe Hall's novel *The Well of Loneliness*, to the "variant" of the fifties, so defined by the founders of the first lesbian organization, "Daughters of Bilitis" who discouraged butch-femme identifications and emphasized "sexual preference". It was the sixties that gave birth to the notion of "sexual orientation", lesbianism being a female version of homosexuality. This was supplanted in the seventies with the equation of lesbianism with feminism and "woman-identified experience" which did not depend on genital desire for another woman. In the nineties "queer politics" emerged—gender-bending, lesbian queers who see themselves more like gay men, and lesbians who have sex with men. Whisman concludes that:

> In the end, a lesbian must simply be any woman who calls herself one, understanding that we place ourselves within that category, drawing and redrawing the boundaries in ever-shifting ways (Whisman, 1993, p. 60).

This paper very usefully highlights the limitations of any theory that offers a definitive account or aetiology of "the lesbian". In psychoanalytic theorizing there is no distinction between the same-sex sexuality between, for example, two upper-class married white women such as Virginia Woolf and Vita Sackville-West in the twenties and that of a black working-class woman who identifies as a lesbian queer contemporaneously. Where distinctions are made, these are in relation to different types of unconscious defence. For example, Limentani specifies three groups of homosexual individuals: those engaged in a flight from the opposite sex, those whose homosexuality serves as a defence against psychotic anxieties and, lastly, the "truly bisexual individuals" whose male and female aspects are dissociated and in whose personalities splitting and multiple identifications are dominant (Limentani, 1989, p. 109).

Foucault's account of the complex interweaving of moral, legal, medical and psychoanalytic discourses and their roles as powerful mechanisms in the construction of sexuality as normal or abnormal continues to be relevant. Psychoanalysts have played a powerful role in the maintenance of laws and restrictions (see Note 1) in relation to homosexuality with their very public pronouncements that it is a pathology. For example, Ismond Rosen from the Institute of Psychoanalysis spoke publicly and on the television in support of Clause 28 (passed as Section 28 in 1988) when it was being debated in parliament. Hannah Segal, who is well-known for her left-wing affiliations and anti-nuclear campaigning, is explicit about her view of lesbian parenting, exclaiming about a baby adopted by a lesbian: "What the hell is going to happen to this boy when he reaches adolescence?" (Segal, 1990, p. 211). For Segal, homosexuality and lesbianism represent an attack on the heterosexual parental couple. Charles Socarides, the American psychoanalyst who was invited in 1995 by the British National Health Service body, the Association of Psychoanalytic Psychotherapy, to deliver its annual lecture publicly campaigned for many years for homosexuality to be reinstated as a pathology by the American Psychiatric Association. In an article in the Washington Times Socarides (1994) argues that homosexuality

> cannot make a society or keep one going for very long. It oper-
> ates against the cohesive elements of society. It drives the sexes

in opposite directions, and no society can long endure when either the child is neglected or the sexes war with each other (Socarides, Washington Times, 1994).

These examples illustrate how psychoanalytic theory, while claiming to be value-free and based on "observation" is, instead, a conflation of medical, legal and moral discourses. A proliferation of psychoanalytic theories have been generated which seek to explain the aetiology of homosexuality but they all rest on the conviction, except in rare cases, that homosexuality can never be fulfilling, satisfying or mature. They also rest on the assumption that sexual-identity can be viewed in isolation from the social context. Such a view does not take into account the diversity of forms of homosexual sex, identities, or relationships. It is in the dimension of sexuality that psychoanalytic theory emerges as so very impoverished. I would emphasize that this impoverishment extends also to accounts of heterosexuality. It is for this reason that it is particularly important for psychoanalytic therapists to look to other sources to extend our own possibilities of thinking about sexuality, to be open to the multiplicity of metaphors that point to the uniqueness of sexual experience and its constantly shifting nature. Philosophical texts are, as I have shown, one important source and another is literature.

In 1982 the black lesbian writer, Audre Lorde (novelist, feminist theorist and poet), published her novel *Zami*. It tells the story of a black woman growing up in Harlem in the thirties and her later life as a black lesbian in the fifties during the McCarthy era. "Zami", writes Lorde, is a Carriacou name for "women who work together as friends and lovers" (Lorde, 1982, p. 255). Lorde's writing is vivid and sensuous and is a testimony to the complexity and diversity of lesbian sexualities. It highlights how same-sex love does not necessarily imply sameness in roles, identities, experiences or cultures. For Lorde, it is "difference" that is always at play. As black, white, butch, femme, young, old, as an oppressed group looking for a place of recognition, pressure on lesbians to form a group identity was strong but, she writes:

Each of us had our own needs and pursuits, and many different alliances. Self-preservation warned some of us that we could not

> afford to settle for one easy definition ... it was a while before
> we came to realize that our place was the very house of differ-
> ence rather than the security of any one particular difference
> (Lorde, 1982, p. 226).

The book contains many moving descriptions of lovemaking
between women. For Lorde, sexuality is not confined to Oedipal
configurations, flowing instead between many different shores:

> I have felt the age-old triangle of mother, father and child,
> with the "I" at its eternal core, elongate and flatten into the ele-
> gantly strong triad of grandmother mother daughter, with the
> "I" moving back and forth, flowing in either or both directions.
> (Lorde, 1982, p. 7).

None of her descriptions can be exhaustively interpreted within
a developmental schema. To attempt to do so would be to miss
the complex interplay of positions that are exchanged and shift
between the lovers. In the following passage it could be interpreted
that there are moments that resonate with the "pre-Oedipal" of
psychoanalytic theorizing: there is reference to need, to hunger,
and to oral pleasure. But such an interpretation does not take
account of the mutual exchange between the lovers, the simulta-
neity of giving and receiving pleasure, the shifting of power back
and forth, the pleasure in the "otherness" of the other lover:

> I dove beneath her wetness, her fragrance, the silky insistence
> of her body's rhythms, illuminating my own hungers ... Her
> body answered the quest of my fingers my tongue my desire
> to know another woman, again and again, until she arched like
> a rainbow, and shaken, I slid back through our heat coming to
> rest upon her thighs. I surfaced dizzy and blessed with her rich
> myrrh taste in my mouth. ... (Lorde, 1982, p. 139).

The importance of Lorde's writing to analysts lies in her acute
sensitivity to the specificity of each of her character's experience, which includes a recognition of the social context and the
way in which discourses on gender, race, class and sexuality
shape this experience. At no point can their experience be pinned

down, assumed or generalized. In the following case presentation I will show how my struggle to be open to my patient's uniqueness and difference whilst recognizing her position(s) within the socio-historical context was crucial in our work.

My relationship with this patient, whom I shall call Gloria, was particularly challenging as she herself longed so much to find an identity or a theory that would name her, explain her, complete her and to which she would "belong". Gloria's own search for explanations and her belief that the achievement of a particular identity would bring her happiness mirror the rigidity of psychoanalytic theorizing that equates maturity with the taking up of a heterosexual identity. For the purposes of this article the presentation is highly condensed, and I will restrict my focus to the aspect of the work that concerned Gloria's preoccupation with her identity.

Gloria was a 29-year-old mixed race woman. She had been born to a white English mother and a Nigerian father who died when she was 18. He was a soldier in the British army and Gloria's early life was spent moving between countries before her family settled in Britain where they moved several more times. Gloria had one older and one younger brother and a younger sister who, she said, was sexually abused by her father. She herself had wondered if she too was an incest survivor. Gloria stormed her way into analysis in a publicly funded centre in which I was working. She wanted to join a group I was running and, since one of the group members knew her, I felt unable to accept her into the group. She responded to my decision with fury, crying and accusing me of being a "fucking white racist", of shutting her out. She said that the other group member "had everything" and that, as a mixed race lesbian, there was never a place for her. As her rage grew, so did my anxiety that she might smash me or my consulting-room up. However, I also felt intrigued by the relentlessness of her demand and I warmed to her fighting spirit. She responded to my offer of a place in individual analysis with guilt—and amazement that the enormity of her fury had failed to drive me to reject her outright. Gloria also said that she had idealized me (since attending a one-day workshop I had run), and this was one aspect of her disappointment in me. She had just failed her degree in nursing. I was the fourth person she had worked with and I saw her once a week for just over three years.

Gloria's quest for her identity concerned her both as a lesbian and as a mixed race woman in white British culture. She often spoke of a highly significant moment in her life: her first memory of being subjected to racism. Aged ten and starting at a new school, she was taunted and stared at, called "wog" and "chocolate drop". She could see the children's lips moving but it was "like a television set with the sound turned down". She could not hear and she could not speak. At home she barricaded herself in her room and, for a whole year after that, she hardly ever went to school. This was Gloria's most vivid memory of direct racism. However, she also expressed a desperation about the lack of recognition she received from her mother who, she felt, was unable to accept her with her dark skin colour, darker than her sister's. Her father's inability to feel any pride in being black and his rejection of his own culture, including his Catholicism, to integrate himself into white English culture were a frequent source of resentment to her.

From the first session when Gloria called me a "fucking white racist", I was acutely aware of my position as a white analyst. In one session in which she was expressing her fury at white people's treatment of her as a black woman, I commented that she was also identifying with how these people saw her. She responded by saying this was because she had no self, she was "nothing". In the following session she admitted that she had been furious with me. She felt that I had implied that she should not fight racism, and that she was "acting like a victim". She ascertained that this was because I was white and therefore could have no understanding of her. At times, in the transference, Gloria assumed I was Jewish in an attempt, I think, to make an alliance with me on the basis that we both must have experienced racism.

That racism can have profound effects on an individual's world (conscious and unconscious) is often dismissed by psychoanalysts and psychoanalytic psychotherapists. Interpretations that acknowledge an individual's experience of racism are deemed to be "a collapse into the sociological". It is claimed that the "deeper level" of the individual's suffering is located within early familial relationships, and it is assumed that such relationships occur in isolation from our racist culture. A Foucauldian analysis, in contrast, recognizes how powerfully racist discourses have penetrated and saturated interpersonal relationships. The main components of racism, those of hostility, devaluation and envy can operate to create a persecutory world that is severely undermining and may even threaten complete annihilation.

Gloria often said "I don't exist", "I have no self", "I am nothing". Her frantic search to find what she called her "real identity" led her to join black women's groups, lesbian groups, incest survivors groups, Alcoholics Anonymous, Sex and Love Addicts Anonymous, Substance Abusers Anonymous, Compulsive Eaters Anonymous, and an organization for dyslexic people. Each of these groups would disappoint and enrage her as she could never totally belong: in each of them she felt that her other identities were not sufficiently recognized; they did not recognise her black identity or her lesbian identity or her disability as dyslexic. The more she searched to belong, the more obliterated she would feel: "It's like fading into the wall, I become as yellow as the wall".

It was crucial that I acknowledge the extent of Gloria's despair and also the specificity of its form: her quest for an identity. It was an important moment in Gloria's therapy when she was able to laugh with recognition at my comment that, even if she did find a mixed race, black lesbian, incest survivors group for drug, eating and alcohol addicts with dyslexia, there would still be something missing. In searching for her identity Gloria sought sameness and totality. This must be distinguished from the taking up of an identity that signifies difference, thus enabling the articulation of the specificity of what may have been denied individually and institutionally by the dominant culture. For Gloria, as yet, to acknowledge her difference was to risk annihilation: "I was like someone being bayoneted", she said of her experience of racism. Gloria's search to belong was frantic, driving her in a relentless thirst for possession: "I could destroy myself to get what I want"; "I thought I was caring, but I don't give a toss about people"; "I need Janet (her lover) as a life-support machine". This was reflected in the transference. In a session after a holiday break early on in her therapy, Gloria declared to me that she was a "batterer" and that she could have killed Janet when she had held her captive in her flat. I asked her whether, in her violence, she also felt angry towards me. She said her "mind had gone blank" and then that she did not want to hurt me. She went on to talk of being obsessed with sex, following a woman on a train whom she wanted to "fuck". She felt she could smash the therapy room up, kill someone or hurt herself; she didn't know where it would end. Gloria's fragility and desperation were compelling her to want to consume me in every possible way, including through sex and through destruction. It was important that I acknowledged the acute intensity of her feelings of vulnerability and powerlessness in my break. However, what emerged as being even more crucial was my statement that I was prepared to work very hard with her to explore the source of her violent feelings, but that, if she was violent, I would stop working with her. She looked visibly relieved and said to me that it was important to her that I was tough like that since, otherwise, she could not move forward. For Gloria it was vital that I acknowledge her violence as a real possibility, not only a fantasy and that it concerned me. It was also important that I insisted on a limit to her fantasies of power and domination, opening out the possibility of reflecting on and moving beyond her violence.

For many months Gloria spoke endlessly, of possession, of wanting to belong, of wanting to find her identity. Her speech was permeated with explanations and interpretations of her behaviour: "That's the needy child, isn't it? That's the need for a mother, isn't it?" I was left feeling unmoved, objectified or non-existent as her words streamed over me, limitlessly. She would describe herself as "being all over the place", "mad", "schizophrenic" and "rambling". My interpretations regarding her desire for possession, the all or nothing quality of her demand, and her experience of gaps and, separation as devastation and rejection were met with agreement followed by explanations and justifications in relation to her past: images of her father, as controlling, manipulative, possessive, evil and mad, and of her mother, as cold and calculating appeared. But it was as if my interpretations and her connections became yet more objects to add to her collection of explanations. At times I would say to her "and how do all these explanations help?" and she would admit, sometimes tearfully, that she needed these to assuage the depth of her despair, yet her search was futile: "It's all labels, isn't it? I've nothing inside ... it's like going into a hole and finding another hole ... there's no substance ... I'm like one of those dolls on a production line without eyes or features". For Gloria necessity or limitation was associated with annihilation. She described this as being "alone, totally alone, in the Antarctic with no clothes and no food, with the wind driving over me, and the cold sea". Her survival was under threat.

After nearly a year in analysis Gloria began a new relationship with a woman, Paula. This was at a point in her analysis when she was exploring the distance between us. My experiences of being bored and non-existent in her presence were becoming much less frequent: I felt more space for my own spontaneity. When I had laughed with her in one session, she told me a few weeks later that she had realized that I was not only cold and authoritarian, as she had thought, but that I could be warm too. She associated this coldness with her mother's rejection of her, contrasting it with her father's possessiveness and eroticization of his relationship with her.

This relationship with Paula was very precious to Gloria. It marked a shift in her ability to reflect on her thirst for totality without being driven to violence. Shortly after it began she talked of being very self-destructive, getting into debt and not turning up at college. She wept, saying "It's to do with my father, I feel I should have done more to keep him alive". He had died when Gloria was nineteen at a time when, she was in trouble owing to drug abuse. She described seeing his dead body on the mortuary slab and of giving him her St Christopher, "my own safekeeping for my own journey". She felt now he was "like a carcass" on her back and she returned to his grave where she burnt photographs of him in an effort to make him die. Instead, his presence as a tantalizing Don Juan figure with access to power and women came to life in the therapy.

Gloria grew terrified that Paula would leave her for a relationship with a man. She would say that she could never really "have" women in the way that men do: she wanted to "have Paula, open her up, get through to her, penetrate her, fuck her, thrust her way into her". She began to wonder at this point too whether she really was an incest survivor, as she could not remember any actual sexual contact with her father. She did, however, recall finding his pornographic magazines and his condoms. She also remembered standing at the top of the stairs provoking her father to be angry, knowing that her mother had forbidden him to hit her and experiencing, as she described it, an erotic excitement in tantalizing him.

In the transference Gloria would, at times, respond to my interpretations with almost masochistic excitement, which she connected with her memory of provoking her father. She would also often flatter me, telling me how good I was as an analyst. "I need to possess to feel real," she would say. During this period, in her efforts to control me, she would miss sessions before and after holiday breaks and wait for me to initiate contact with her.

As Gloria's anger towards men increased she fantasized about shooting them with a machine-gun, since they had the power she craved, including the power to take Paula from her and to exploit her as a woman as well. When a man jostled her on the tube she felt she was losing control. She was fighting for her life: "There is no oxygen, it's like swimming and never reaching the shore or nearly getting there and the oxygen supply is taken off your back". Images of her mother as suffocating emerged: "my mother plays mind games, I used to think she was a witch, she messes things up and she's destructive. It's because of her I feel so insecure". She expressed disappointment that even her father's death did not bring her closer to her.

Gradually, in the third year of her analysis, Gloria was realizing the limits of her quest. Periods of fury were interspersed with moving sessions in which Gloria wept, admitting feeling "battle-worn", recognizing how for so long her fighting had protected her from her terror of annihilation, of being reduced to nothing. At times her distress at the racism she experienced on the graphics diploma course she embarked on fifteen months into her therapy threatened to destroy her: "It's like an endless spiral towards death"; she felt "like an ant that is going to be crushed" in the face of another student, but she managed to continue. Her relationship with Paula, although turbulent, also survived and they managed to move into a new home together.

Gloria was able to acknowledge how she was changing and to look back at the enormity of her aggression, at how she "would grow huge and ugly, my shoulders would grow big and my words would come out of a sewer". She felt, as a result of her analysis, that something different was emerging, "but I don't know how to be that yet". "As if you don't have a language?" I asked her. "Yes, that's exactly it, I don't have the words". When she began her analysis Gloria would say "words have no meaning, they don't permeate my brain", and that it was as if other people were "speaking a foreign language". Eighteen months into her analysis she said that in speaking to me she was now beginning to "feel real". She said, "It's like the Channel

Tunnel, a channel of communication, and you're opening out the other end of it".

In my work with Gloria I learned how crucial it was that I didn't subscribe to simplistic notions of identity and collude with her belief that she would be able to find her real identity. Instead, it was crucial that I saw how this search constrained her and served as a defence against her overwhelming fears of annihilation. It was only as she was able to realize the contingency of identities that she began to find her own voice from within her many different positions of difference. In not being as compelled to possess she was able to begin to find an intimacy that could allow for the other's difference.

My work with Gloria highlights how the significance of particular identities, such as being lesbian, being black, being a woman, or being working-class can be constantly shifting and are often intertwined. Gloria's search for her "real" identity arose from a desperate need to defend herself against her terror of annihilation. However, the way in which her identities as black and lesbian found articulation is also historically specific. It is hard to imagine a patient speaking of herself in this way even as recently as the 1960s (see Whisman, 1993, above).

A Foucauldian analysis allows for an interpretation, which does not presuppose a split between the psychic and the socio-political. Such an approach contrasts with a traditional psychoanalytic approach: here the concern would be with Gloria's violence and depression as acultural and ahistorical and as "underlying" her defensive search for her identity. A recognition of the historical specificity of Gloria's search and the identities she took up extends our understanding of her struggle: the conscious and unconscious impact of racism on her, the dynamics of desire between her father and herself and her relation to her mother as a girl/woman within the context of white patriarchal culture, her search as a lesbian for intimacy with a woman which could allow for mutuality and difference. Her terror of annihilation was rooted within the interplay of these various socio-cultural factors.

My next case illustration is an account of analytic work with a very different patient, a white, married man whom I shall call Derek. As in my work with Gloria, I was not concerned with an analysis of the "causes" of his homosexuality in terms of intra-psychic dynamics, with a view to his moving towards a more stable heterosexual identity. Instead, I aimed to be attentive to the particular conscious and unconscious meanings his body and his sexuality had for him within the wider social context, the discourses of his family, his class background, Christianity, medicine, and contemporary gay culture. As with my account of my work with Gloria, I will show the importance of an approach that does not presuppose a split between the psychic and the social.

Derek was in his late forties. When he arrived at his first session he had a grey, almost mechanical demeanour. He was immaculately dressed in a city suit, a conventional persona that masked an enormous conflict that pervaded his life. Derek lived in Berkshire with his wife Sally and their teenage daughter. Sally was a housewife who also did some voluntary work for a local charity. Derek was a stockbroker who did regular workouts in the gym. Sally's mother lived near them and was closely involved with their lives.

In the past year Derek had been in a private psychiatric unit for two short spells and had been prescribed anti-depressants which he had recently stopped taking. What had preoccupied Derek and caused him terrible anguish, he shared with me with obvious trepidation, was that he was gay. He had known this, he said, since he was about eleven. At twenty he had had a brief relationship with a man and, a few years later, he had got married in the hope of putting his homosexuality well behind him. After some years he began to cottage (have sex in public toilets) occasionally in his lunch-hours. For the past two years he had had a relationship with a man, Peter, of which his wife was unaware. Three years before, he and Sally had attended marriage guidance counselling for a short time offered by a Christian organization (Derek was a committed Catholic), but Derek hadn't felt sufficiently understood by the counsellor. After that they had tried to "meet half way" by making an agreement that, two evenings a week, he would be allowed to go out to gay bars. This had had not lasted very long because Derek could not bear to see the distress he felt that he was causing Sally. Sally now thought things were "back to normal" and that Derek's depression was a medical condition.

In this first session Derek wanted reassurance that I was not someone who would try to change him that I didn't think that his being gay meant that there was something wrong with him. A psychiatrist at the hospital had told him that it was "all to do with his relationship with his mother". He had once talked to a priest who was reputed to be gay and had been told that his being gay need not stop him from being a Christian, but Derek was unsure about this.

In the first sessions Derek was very tentative when he talked about his sexuality yet, simultaneously, he conveyed a desperate need to do so. He would return again and again to the effect of his homosexuality on his wife, terrified that she would be, as he said, "destroyed" or become ill with distress. Derek's mother had died from cancer when he was fourteen and he felt that he had never really mourned her. He felt that his father's and younger brother's grief had taken precedence. Derek recognized that there was a connection between his fears about Sally and his relationship to his mother. As the analysis unfolded he realized how much he had longed to please his mother, how he had always felt that she favoured his younger brother.

Gradually Derek began to talk about his feelings about his own body, the birthmark on his back, his shoulders being "at a tilt" (which was not visible to me). His mother had been ill when he was born; he thought that she had nearly died and that his birth had caused it. Memories emerged of his being in the bath and his mother's intrusive obsession with his cleanliness making him sure there was something "wrong" with his body. I suggested that his workouts in the gym were a way of trying to make his body his own. He said that he thought there was something in that; after a workout he would feel momentarily relaxed and good about himself.

In the transference it seemed that I represented an accepting mother, but this was threatening too. On one occasion I had to change his appointment to a later time and there was to be a gap between his leaving work and his appointment with me. He realized that he would probably spend this time in a gay bar and his guilt about coming to our sessions surfaced; he felt that being in analysis was to indulge himself, that if I could accept him, what on earth would that lead to. He felt that the analysis was a betrayal of Sally, that, although not secret, it was not having the effect that she hoped for, namely that he would be cured of his depression and so would no longer need to fantasize that being gay would be a way out. Their marriage could be saved.

Derek would often refer to his "wild side". It was then that the greyness would momentarily leave his face, his eyes would shine and he would laugh, turning his face away in embarrassment. I interpreted to him that, however terrifying it was that Sally might be destroyed, he also needed her as a way of constraining the wildness he feared. My interpretations regarding his fury with her were met with resistance. It was hard for him to recognize the aggression he directed towards Sally through his dramatic depressions and allusions to suicide, martyring himself to tell her "look what you are doing to me". His suicidal thoughts were very real to him; he would examine different ways of dying in detail; most of all he wished he could just go to sleep and never wake up. These feelings were heightened in the weeks leading up to the family holiday, but they were also a response to his beginning to face the strength of his own desire. I was extremely concerned about him and very aware of his precariousness. How could he live if to live was to destroy the other? His birth had nearly killed his mother, and her death when he was fourteen had provided evidence that she could not survive his growing independence from her.

In one session he experimented with an alternative solution. He came into the session and threw himself into the chair, his head bent and his arm covering his face: "I'm throwing in the towel", he said dramatically. He had contacted a Christian organization that would offer him counselling to help him be free of his homosexuality. I suggested to him that in taking flight from his conflict he was also attacking himself, that he was depriving himself of the possibility of desire or pleasure in his life. In this session more images of his mother emerged, particularly of her exhaustion and his fear that she would literally wear out. At home the atmosphere had been grey, void of any fun or spontaneity, with his father's depression always "down on things". This was just how life was, but Derek could see it was different in other families. Derek's parents were working class and they lived on an estate that bordered on a middle-class area. Derek always felt that he could never be as smart as the middle-class children; he was very much inscribed in a discourse in which, as a working-class child, he was designated as inferior, as not-having, of being deprived and unworthy of what other, financially better-off people had access to. Alongside other aspects, Derek's position within discourses on class played an important role in relation to the question of his entitlement to his own desires.

Derek often spoke of Catholicism and perhaps for me, as a non-Christian, it was here that my own openness to difference was especially challenged. It was crucial that I allow Derek to find his own way in trying to integrate his homosexuality with his faith. Since Derek had been raised as a Catholic, those Christian discourses that designated homosexuality as a sin had been very influential in shaping his sexuality. Similarly, his decision to marry had arisen from his exposure to Christian discourses that hold marriage to be sacrosanct, a commitment before God, for life. To be homosexual was to be lured by the devil and he would describe horrifying fantasies of being in the devil's grip. The Christian notion of heaven was also a strong feature in his fears of change: over a number of sessions in which he talked about his mother's death, he realized how he had been saving himself for his mother in the after-life. Ever since she had died he had comforted himself with the thought that they would see each other again. He had therefore tried to preserve himself as the son she would have wanted, suspending his own life. For Derek, to live was to be for another.

Six months after Derek began therapy, a place came up for him and Sally at a couples counselling service. Derek would report on every session, puzzled by how much the counsellor would focus on Sally as if she, or at least her difficulty in accepting Derek's homosexuality, was the problem. He was amazed that, although she was extremely upset, she was not "destroyed". He battled with his wish for her permission in order to legitimize his own feelings. Each session he would risk more, being able to tell her finally that he had to follow his feelings. Together they decided that he should go out one night a week and see how that worked. The couples counsellor was sceptical but Derek felt positive. Unlike their previous attempt at a compromise this arrangement represented a real turning point. Derek was able to tell Sally that there was no going back.

It became clear that Derek was already much more involved in the gay scene than he was able to tell me at the beginning, albeit restricted to the daytime. He had several long-standing phone contacts and a special contact address for gay men he was in correspondence with. He felt a particular affinity with gay prisoners, identifying with their experience of imprisonment, forming a particularly intense postal relationship with a convicted murderer who was gay. As well as seeing Peter, he would have other encounters with gay men who would respond to his ads; "Married city gent seeks wild time with leather gays/skinheads". He spoke with great fondness of a young skinhead with whom he would occasionally have sex. He was a biker who lived in a darkened room lit with discotheque lights and packed with disco equipment. We talked of his attraction to what he longed to express himself that was associated with toughness, spontaneity, wildness.

It was only after about eight months in analysis that Derek was able to talk more freely about a crucial aspect of this "wildness". He warned me that there was something important that he had yet to tell me, but it was very embarrassing. Also, he was afraid that, in talking about it, the excitement of it would disappear. It was a story that began in his childhood when he was seven years old. At school he was terrified of the boys' toilets with its rushing water and bad smells. He would rarely use them, managing to hold on until he got home at lunchtime or after school. One day, in a school assembly, he was desperate to go to the toilet. Too terrified to go he weighed up that it would be less terrible just to wet himself there and then: others hadn't been severely told off for their "accidents". However, when he got up, leaving the wet puddle, the consequences were enormous. He was publicly reprimanded by the headmistress and his mother was furious with him when he returned home. He felt utterly humiliated. Up until she died his mother would keep reminding him when to go to the toilet.

When Derek started to masturbate he would recall this event in detail in a way that would arouse him, urinating in the family bathroom to achieve climax. He would recalculate endlessly just how much urine had been left on the floor at school and what it would have looked like. This fantasy had continued to dominate his adult sexual life, and he would masturbate in the same way when his wife and daughter were out. He admitted that he was very attracted to the notion of "watersports" (sex with urination) with another man; this was the wildness that really terrified him and he felt that, if he allowed full pleasure in his homosexuality, this would have to include watersports. At the same time, he mused tentatively, could it be that there wasn't anything wrong with this if he could meet someone who was, as he said, "like-minded". He had confided in the skinhead but this man had not experienced anything similar.

It was crucial in this session that I just listened quietly. It seemed at the beginning that at any moment he might stop, delaying his revelation for another time. To speak of this aspect of his sexuality was such an enormous leap of faith and I was touched by the combination of terror and urgency in his voice. My openness to witnessing every detail of his story was absolutely vital and, in particular, my openness to its personal meaning for him. I made no effort in this session to make connections, to make it all understandable, to risk tidying it all up. It was important that this long-hidden story could just stand between us and be witnessed by us both.

In the next session and in later sessions we talked of how this fantasy had been a way of reworking his humiliating experience, of finding a way of being in control, his pleasure assuaging his feelings of humiliation, his finding potency in the face of these. It was essential that I was able to suspend notions of normality and pathology, to allow the uniqueness of Derek's experience to speak. My interpretations and connections were not made with a view to defusing the fantasy, to return him to a kind of mature homosexuality. Rather they were to flesh out the less conscious meaning that the fantasy had for him, allowing him to choose.

Several months after Derek's disclosure, his relationship with Peter ended. Shortly after, he formed a relationship with a young man, John, who was involved with someone else. For the first months they were sexually involved but, after a particularly intense and intimate sexual experience, John decided he could no longer be disloyal to his partner. Derek was very sad and disappointed about this but continued to enjoy and to be deeply committed to their friendship. John was a literary theorist and opened up a new world for Derek: he described his wife's puzzlement at the living- room table being piled high with poetry books and plays from the library. Derek also started to write his own poetry and occasionally brought them to sessions.

John was then appointed to a job outside London but they made plans for their friendship to continue. The emotional intimacy that Derek enjoyed with John was very new to him. There was an honesty and aliveness in it that Derek did not share with his wife. We discussed how it was no coincidence that John was not available to him sexually: this would be too risky, partly because such a situation would mean having to take a decision about leaving his wife, a decision that would take him a long time to find the courage to do. It might also mean he would be vulnerable to being again enslaved to the demands of another. Now, in the transference, it was the analysis that was making these demands, taking up too much time, making his week's schedule too tight. However, Derek's mechanical demeanour was being shed: his face and body had become more alive and expressive as he began to find a way to expand and move without constantly fearing the destruction of his mother.

From time to time Derek would think about the possibility of experimenting with watersports with other gay men, but with a relaxed thoughtfulness, none of the compulsiveness, and much less shame. In listening to him I was very aware that a traditional psychoanalytic view would hold firmly to the view that Derek's desires to participate in watersports, however consensual, must be pathological in every aspect. Such a perspective forecloses on possibilities of sexuality that are not related to sexual reproduction. In contrast, within contemporary gay culture, watersports and many other sexual practices are regarded as acceptable, provided they are consensual and pleasurable. From a Foucauldian viewpoint such practices are culturally specific; they do not arise out of a repressed sexuality that is located outside culture. In my work with Derek it was important that I held both positions simultaneously. Derek's pleasure had connections with his past experience of urinating publicly as a child, yet I also was concerned to hold open the possibility of watersports as a sexual practice that does not in itself have to be a symptom of psychopathology. Why, for example, should watersports be regarded as a symptom whilst other practices, such as oral sex, are regarded as being within the range of "normal" sexual practices for heterosexuals within the West? In the nineteenth century arguments were waged within psychiatry and medicine as to whether masturbation was a symptom of disturbance or disease. What informs our views on what is normal or healthy, and what is abnormal and deviant?

My aim in this chapter has been to raise questions regarding the way in which we as analysts attend to the specificity of our patients' experiences. What are the values that we bring to our listening? Is it necessary to presuppose a split between the psychic and the social? In showing how a Foucauldian perspective can be combined with a psychoanalytic approach, I have demonstrated how this can increase our sensitivity to the cultural specificity of our patients' speech. I have shown how questions of identity in relation to sexual orientation are intertwined with those of race and class. They also arise out of a multiplicity of shifting discourses including the legal, religious, medical and the colonial. I have emphasized that, to truly engage with the complexity of our patients' experiences in their conscious and unconscious aspects, we must have the courage to suspend any temptation to simplify, to universalize and to colonize. As Gayatri Spivak, the cultural theorist, points out:

> For me, the question "Who should speak?" is less crucial than "Who will listen?" "I will speak for myself as a Third World person" is an important position for political mobilization today. But the real demand is that, when I speak from that position, I should be listened to seriously; not with that kind of benevolent imperialism, really, which simply says that because I happen to be an Indian or whatever ... When they want to hear an Indian speaking as an Indian. ... they cover over the fact of the ignorance that they are allowed to possess, into a kind of homogenization (Spivak, 1990, pp. 59–60).

Note

1. Such restrictions have included a differing age of consent for gay men (as compared with heterosexuals), the threat to lesbian mothers of the loss of the custody of their children, and restricted access to artificial insemination for lesbians because it has been supposed that they cannot offer an emotionally healthy upbringing for their children. This has changed considerably in the UK, reflected in the passing of the Civil Partnership Act 2004, but it is only as recently as 2000 that the age of consent for gay men was lowered to sixteen in line with heterosexuals.

   Section 28 was a bill passed in 1988 prohibiting the "promotion" of homosexuality and the teaching of the acceptability of homosexuality as a "pretended family relationship". This law was eventually, after a long campaign, repealed in 2003.

CHAPTER THREE

Is Melanie Klein the one who knows who you really are?

Noreen O'Connor

Any social theory whether focussed on a group or an individual inevitably embodies value judgements. This is also true of different psychoanalytic theories, notwithstanding claims for truth based on the "explanation" of psychic "facts". In this chapter I raise the question of the normative character of Kleinian psychoanalysis. Melanie Klein's genius was to have charted the desolate hinterland of psychosis; going beyond discrete conceptions of the life and death instinct she explores the soma/ psychic territory of anxieties, persecution, splitting, loss, disintegration, phantasy. By thematising psychotic states or "positions" Klein developed psychoanalytic technique such that it has seriously challenged psychiatry's pretension to total "expertise" in this area and she also challenges the primacy of pharmacological treatments of psychosis. Her work also calls psychoanalysts from resting in a false sense of being at home in the world with our patients, that is, from the security of making facile transference interpretations, towards a greater sensitivity to the depth of phantasies and of the symbolisation of pain and suffering.

Philosophers have, for thousands of years in different cultures, urged people to pay attention to that which is taken for granted in their day-to-day struggle to survive in order that they can live their lives more fully, more happily. Philosophers, however, are aware that such exhortations are based on their particular claims to know "reality", the "human", what is "just". Philosophers, like psychoanalysts, do claim to provide reflections and practices which change people's lives and even societies, but while they do not claim to be scientists, they do acknowledge the importance of competing theories and are open to questions regarding their claims.

To highlight my task of elucidating some normative features of Kleinian psychoanalysis I raise the following questions: why is Kleinian psychoanalysis so popular in Britain? Why is psychoanalysis so often split off from philosophy, from thoughtfulness and critical appraisal? Does Kleinian psychoanalysis make claims for truth? What kinds of claims does it make regarding its technique?

Do any of these questions matter in practice—if it works and brings the lost fragmented bits of the "self" towards the warm comfort of fitting together? Is Kleinian theory phallocentric (is the breast a symbol of the penis or vice versa)? Is it ethnocentric, homophobic? My strategy is not to follow in a formal manner each of these questions and risk foreclosing issues; rather, to hold them open as guides in order to crystallise the implications of Kleinian psychoanalysis for, particularly, the theorising of gender identity and sexual identity whether heterosexual, lesbian, gay or asexual.

In "The Psycho-Analytic Play Technique: Its History and Significance", Klein (1955, p. 138) succinctly expresses her project of tracing impulses, anxieties and phantasies back to their "origin" which are the feelings towards the mother's breast; she argues that object-relations almost begin at birth and furthermore, that *all* aspects of mental life are bound up with object-relations.

Recourse to biologistic arguments is clearly exemplified in Klein's account of the development of gender identity. She specifies the very early identification with the mother by boys and girls as the "femininity phase" (Klein, 1948, p. 205). This phase, she argues, has its basis in the anal-sadistic level and imparts a new content such that faeces become equated with the child that is longed for. As with all of her developmental stages or positions the femininity phase has its characteristic anxiety, in this case it is related to the womb and the father's penis (Klein, 1952, p. 81). The first persecutory objects, external and internal, are the mother's bad breast and father's bad penis. Genital desires towards both parents at around the age of six months initiate the Oedipus complex and are initially intertwined with oral, anal and urethral desires and phantasies of a libidinal and aggressive nature: "As in the castration complex of girls, so in the femininity complex of the male, there is at bottom the frustrated desire for a special organ." (Klein, 1948, p. 206).

With the onset of the Oedipus complex Klein acknowledges the girl's awareness of the vagina and of genital sensations but she maintains that "onanism" does not give girls as adequate an outlet for these excitations as it does boys. Consequently the accumulated lack of gratification is another reason for complications and disturbances of female sexual development. One major obstacle to the girl's development is that while the boy actually possesses the penis which enables him to enter into rivalry with the father, the girl has only the unsatisfied desire for motherhood. The girl's castration complex is felt as dread of injury to her womanhood and this causes her to over-estimate greatly the penis which she lacks. Klein concludes that the reason why women adorn and beautify themselves is because they want to restore the damaged "comeliness" which originates in anxiety and guilt. Klein then states that penis-envy accounts for the prominent part jealousy plays in so many women's lives. She does not question her own "research findings" regarding the pathological character of female development.

Klein argues that there are two forms of anxiety that all children go through, namely, the fear of being devoured, of being poisoned, castrated, the fear of attacks on the "inside" of the body—these are persecutory anxiety; all anxieties regarding loved objects are grouped under depressive anxiety (Klein, 1950, p.45). The principal anxiety in women is persecutory but also has depressive elements; it is the girl's fear that the dreaded mother will attack her body and the babies it contains. The kind of anxiety expressed by the adult patient is an indication as to what early "psychotic position" of the patient's psyche it belongs.

Klein's exploration of pre-Oedipal, pre-linguistic, object relations led her to prioritise notions of symbolisation and phantasy. She postulates symbolism as the foundation of all sublimation and talents because, she argues, it is by means of symbolic equation that things, activities and interests become the subject of libidinal phantasies (Klein, 1930, p. 237). Klein assumes that there is an "inner" world and an "outer" world and much of her theory construction is concerned with linking them. Her notion of subjectivity is that of an isolated monad rather like Descartes' introspective self who never knows whether he knows or not. What would her theory have been like if she had not assumed a split between "inner" and "outer"? Can we "understand" and work with psychosis without necessarily describing our work in the language of psychosis?

For Klein the subject's relation to the outside world and reality is founded on symbolisation. She stresses the importance of a balance between anxiety, which initiates symbol formation and phantasy, and a capacity for anxiety tolerance on the part of the ego. In the course of presenting her clinical material of her work with a little boy, Dick, she (1930, pp. 243–244) explains how he discovered that a wash-basin symbolised his mother's body; in his phantasy faeces, urine and penis stood for objects with which to attack mother's body, but were also felt as a source of injury to himself.

Klein provides clear statements regarding the necessary pathology of homosexuality. She (1950) cites what she terms the "well-known" criteria for the termination of analysis as: an established potency and heterosexuality, capacity for love, object-relations and work and certain characteristics of the ego which make for mental stability and are bound up with adequate defences. Klein praises Freud for showing the vital relevance of a girl's relationship to her mother for her subsequent relations to men. A girl's homosexual attitude may be reinforced when envy of the mother's breast has been transferred to the father's penis. Also if there are excessive anxieties and conflicts around the oral relation there can be a flight from breast to penis but this does not lead to a stable relation to the penis. Homosexuality may be based on a need to find a good object rather than the avoided primal object: "The fact that such people—and this applies to men as well as to women—can have good object relations is therefore often deceptive. The underlying envy towards the primal object is split off but remains operative and is liable to disturb any relations" (Klein, 1957, p. 200). Klein maintains that female homosexuality is the result of deep disturbance in the oral relation and prevents the experience of full genital orgasm.

The Kleinian mission of establishing a meta-psychology which "knows" the "truth" of sexuality and particularly homosexuality and lesbianism is well represented by Donald Meltzer. He claims that his meta-psychology transcends the medical model of illness and cure. Meltzer specifies the task of psychoanalysis as research into human mentality. Like Klein he is fascinated by the notions of origin and foundation:

> The foundation, in the unconscious of the sexual life of the mature person is the highly complicated sexual relation of the internal parents, with whom he is capable of a rich introjective identification in both masculine and feminine roles ... The penis of the father, with testes, is felt to have a reparative role in which the semen is the essential factor" (Meltzer, 1967, p. xiv).

Meltzer claims to provide a meta-psychological nosology of sexual pathology to replace the descriptions of neuropsychiatry. He argues in favour of a definite act of coition which is "serious" (Meltzer, 1979, p. 84). He describes it as work rather than play and has a sense of urgency related to stresses of the day, week, era; it is an introjective identification of cosmic scope which takes hold of the mind-body. Homosexuality is relegated to the realm of play, foreplay rather than the real thing. Meltzer argues that a term such as "homosexual" can now be given a clear meta-psychological significance. His claim to be innovative in this area is based on his view that homosexuality is not simply located in terms of infantile bisexuality but is situated instead in terms of the polymorphous and perverse which have definitive reference to good and bad sexuality. Meltzer classifies homosexuality as a perversion but stresses that there can be many different causes such as, for example, narcissistic disorder (sado-masochistic wishes), defences against depressive anxieties, infantile zonal confusions.

Hanna Segal, another contemporary Kleinian analyst dedicated to the development of Kleinian theory and practice, is particularly interested in creativity and symbolisation. In *Delusion, Artistic Creativity and Other Psychoanalytic Essays* Segal explains Klein's theory of symbol formation. She characterises symbolising as a three-term relation, between the thing symbolised, the thing functioning as a symbol and the person for whom one represents the other. Symbolisation is an activity of the ego and disturbances in the ego's relation to objects is reflected in disturbances of ego formation. Symbols are created in the *internal* world in order to re-create the original object: "... for the artist, the work of art is his most complete and satisfactory way of allaying the guilt and despair arising out of the depressive position and of restoring his lost objects ..." (Segal, 1981, p. 198).

Segal cites Dilthey's notion of understanding as re-living emotional states as relevant to the artistic endeavour; it is noteworthy that she ignores all twentieth-century advances in hermeneutic theory which systematically criticise divisions between thought and language and spatial metaphors of "inside" and "outside" arising from that dualistic split. Segal (1981, p. 63) summarises her interpretation of Klein's view of the relationship between experience and language. The child has an experience and the mother provides the word or phrase which "contains", encompasses and expresses the meaning. The word provides a container for the meaning. The infant can then internalise this word or phrase containing the meaning.

"Psychoanalysis belongs to the great scientific traditions of freeing thought from dogma, whether religious or arising out of an established scientific tradition itself" (Segal, 1981, p. 217). Segal does not acknowledge what was of crucial significance for Dilthey and subsequent hermeneutical theorists, namely, the historical, perspectival, and value-laden implications in every human endeavour—an issue which has been notably addressed by social scientists. The "scientific" nature of psychoanalysis rests on the claim that psychoanalytic insight initiates change. In order to have this insight one must, in Segal's view, have conscious knowledge of archaic processes that structured one's internal world and conditioned one's perceptions.

Juliet Mitchell (1986), in her introduction to *The Selected Melanie Klein*, praises Klein's work as a new departure in the theory of mental processes. Mitchell comments on Klein's move to Britain and explains how British empirical traditions of direct and careful observation fostered an open-mindedness precluded by over-arching philosophical theories. Mitchell concludes that Klein's empirical open-mindedness coincided with this laudable ethos of British investigation. Mitchell does not refer to the self-justifying character of psychoanalytic conceptualisation nor does she elaborate on what is meant by the term empirical—an issue widely debated by British philosophers and scientists for many centuries. "Clinical" description may be regarded as empirical but claims for explanation based on *a priori* assumptions of instincts, drives, anxieties, can scarcely be considered to be empirical. Does Kleinian psychoanalysis allow for competing theories in the explanation of data or is it making a comprehensive truth claim regarding the necessity of its own methods and "discoveries" of the psyche?

Mitchell offers a fascinating comparison of Freud and Klein. She argues that for Freud repression is a defence that creates a past and a symptom is a return to that past: Klein is concerned with defences without a dimension of time, thus focussing more on atemporal inhibitions of the ego rather than on the symptom. Klein's concern with the pre-Oedipal child and the psychotic is a concern for the spatial where present and past are one; she is not concerned with regression. Mitchell describes Klein's model as a two-way process from inner to outer and back again. She argues that Klein is not a scientific theorist in the nineteenth-century tradition, that is, she does not explain the present by the past. Mitchell (1986, p. 28) then characterises Klein's methods of investigation as "maternal" in the sense that she identifies and intuits on the basis of accumulated experience.

Perhaps one reason for the popularity of Kleinian psychoanalysis is that it fits in with mainstream foundational theories in Western culture dominated by ideals of technology. By "foundational" I mean theories which rely on a set of *a priori*, assumed, or believed set of terms or principles to explain all consequent, subsequent, deduced, or inferred conclusions. Foundational theories frequently make factual claims, such as Klein's claims for the universality of psychic "positions", and then proceed to make value judgements on the basis of such claimed "facts", such as Klein's statements about the centrality of jealousy in women's lives being caused by penis envy. Kleinian psychoanalysis exemplifies the Western ideal of "self-possession", the ideal of retrieving one's origins and being whole and complete in an eternal present. Every aspect of the "psyche" is thematised and known by the privileged expert, there is an operative denial of difference, otherness, diachrony. Psychoanalysis has long been praised for its daring in showing us that the value of human discourse is not confined to the atemporality of logical relations but, as we have seen, Juliet

Mitchell presents Klein in just such terms. François Roustang's comments on Freud are equally relevant to Klein:

> Freud ... pretends to have founded his theory—more precisely his meta-psychology—in universal terms that make it independent of experience. Analysts and patients are therefore both subjected to the laws of this third party who prohibits them from being content with each other's reflection. Either the theory, particularly the meta-psychology, is independent of experience and therefore unverifiable ... or the theory is taken from experience and is therefore only the description or the more or less structured account of it through a new and more appropriate terminology (Roustang, 1983, p. 39).

Highlighting the normativeness of Kleinian psychoanalysis involves a critique of the project of meta-psychology as well as the practice of pathologising. Feminists have been struggling for a long time in their own cultures and families, with basic crucial issues such as food, children, work, racism, violence against women, wars. Such collective struggles have brought great strength, love, and creativity. But what happens when despite the political/personal discoveries there are the disappointments not just with the government, the multi-nationals, with men, when the lesbian feminist is screaming abuse at her lover and feels she is in an endless hell with no more discoveries possible; when the march is over and the woman is again enclosed in that icy coldness which cannot be touched; what happens when the despair weighs her like heavy treacle and she is stuck to the bed; what happens when she feels nothing and all the food in the fridge cannot bring her to life; what happens when she smiles and laughs and is deafened by the song of her horrible fat body, her disgusting self that has to be hidden?

If she is in a privileged context the woman can decide to go to a psychoanalyst so that she can "get to the root of things". A woman analyst and the relief at last that someone recognises the crazy "psychotic bits"; weary of being strong, independent and gay she can be dependent and despairing—the sort of crazy baby that she had never even suspected was the cause of her deadness. And, most of all, the relief that the analyst knows the terrain, the twists and murky cul-de-sacs of the psyche. The analyst, who knows the unbearable blackness, the deadness of the void, the acuity of the nails driven in the brain, the sheer riveting terror of not knowing what is real and what is not, can help.

Does the fact that she is lesbian affect how she will be analysed? One could say that each analysis is individual, which is true, so is it irrelevant to ask about the relevance of one's sexuality? Yet psychoanalysis is centrally a discourse of sexuality and its meaning in our lives—there are volumes lining the libraries of institutes and clinics explaining and exploring the topic of "sexuality". Now we come to the gap which we should mind, that is, the gap between the claim by analysts for the uniqueness and specificity of each analysis and the theories—whether on a medical, scientific or meta-psychological level—which pathologise lesbian and homosexual desires and relationships *per se*, that is, irrespective of other areas of sadness, distress, or difficulty in one's life the fact that one's lover or desire for one is of the same sex is interpreted as deviant, perverse, regardless of other qualities of desire or relationship. Donald Meltzer addresses the gap: "Nothing could be more dangerous than a splitting between the 'doing' of analytical work and the 'talking' about it" (Meltzer, 1967, p. xi). One can conclude from this that lesbians and gay men are automatically pathologised in their analyses or else there is serious inconsistency between psychoanalytic theory and practice.

Why bother with psychoanalysis—human development reduced to the language of drives, relationships between objects or bits of objects? Feminists are aware of the dangers of Freudian phallocentrism and ethnocentrism and have either tended to reject psychoanalysis completely as destructive of women or else have jumped into it and tried to remodel it, according primacy to female development, but not questioning the Oedipal as the developmental benchmark. This is analogous to Christian believers developing a feminist theology. The difference is that Christians stress the centrality of belief and psychoanalysts generally argue in terms of knowledge. But the crucial common issue is that the terms of reference remain within the system. If you don't believe in Christ then you don't know what I'm talking about, if you haven't been in analysis then you don't know what it's about but, of course, you can only know that by acknowledging that I (the analyst) know. When you are in it you know and then you can move around within the discourse.

You might be an old-style type clinging to drives or more radically exploring positions even earlier than the paranoid-schizoid, but there is the shared "knowledge" that what can "cure" is "knowledge" of the developmental stages and/or positions. As Meltzer writes in *The Psychoanalytical Process*:

> It is difficult to imagine that the present book could ... have significance for anyone who has not experienced the analytical process at first hand as a patient ... technical terms employed are well known in the Kleinian literature such as splitting and idealisation, projective identification, internal objects etc ... Less familiar terms are "toilet-breast", "toilet-mummy", "feeding breast", "little boy part of the self" (Meltzer, 1967, p. viii).

I am challenging the self-referential nature of psychoanalysis. Many psychoanalytic institutes have not opened their doors easily to philosophers or to lesbians and gay men (see Ellis, 1994) yet they pronounce themselves to be experts on their desires and love. Psychoanalysts argue for necessary as well as significant conditions for pathologising. In talking about homosexuality they are talking about their "expertise", views of being human, views of reality and claims about the truth and falsity of sexuality—the normal. In fact they are engaged in a discourse about science, pragmatism, morality and politics. I think it is important that there is a dialogue between psychoanalysts and philosophers, feminists, gay men, people who by virtue of their place in society question established norms and practices. People who go to analysis are questioning their lives: why are they desolate, isolated, dead, terrified, hated; is life worth living? How can I talk to people? Hear them? Why can't I work? Who loves me? Is there a god? What is truth? What is real? Do I know anything?

My aim is to invite discussion, not to destroy or to dismiss psychoanalysis nor to confine it by a sociological critique. Psychoanalysis can be very useful in terms of widening our notions as to what constitutes meaningful expression and offering us a way to begin to explore our lives outside of the confines of experiences defined chronologically. I am not advocating the establishment of an "alternative system" of analysis to replace those I criticise. Rather, I am concerned to question any system that claims to have all the answers and be the "one-true" church so to speak. Positions based on necessary conditions do not allow for competing theories or differences. I am attempting to explore not just the institution or the content of psychotherapy but rather the complex matrices that unravel *how* it is practised. Of course, as analysts, we interpret, make connections. But what we think about happiness and reality does matter.

Klein's position on language also matters in psychoanalytic practice. Her theory of symbolisation focuses on a few fundamental somatic symbols such as breast, penis, anus, urethra, faeces, to which all of human expression is ultimately reduced. Wittgenstein's critique of Freud's analysis of dreams can be fruitfully related to Klein's arguments on "early" psychotic positions which, as it were, "remain" in the psyche and are triggered off by later adult experiences. This is an analysis of intentionality which relies on a later reaction caused in daily life by a later situation. What is implied is that the later reaction not only points to the original desire or meaning but is a logically necessary and sufficient condition of the truth of the statement that the person originally desired or meant a particular thing or things (Wittgenstein, 1978, pp. 41–43). Klein's theory of language involves, as I mentioned, a separation of thought from language. She postulates an "outside" world of reality of shared language and an "inner" world of mechanisms without language but mysteriously available to "knowledge". For Klein meaning can exist outside of linguistic practices. This is in line with many essentialist, universalist, foundational theories. In the following chapter (Chapter Four) I argue in favour of the development of an analytic practice within the context of a postmodernist model of communication which acknowledges differences yet allows for the uniqueness and irreducibility of each person's discourse.

The an-arche of psychoanalysis

Noreen O'Connor

In my analytic practice one of my principal concerns is that of allowing for plurality of expressions—the speech of individuals which is irreducible to a unified rationality. This is a concern to maintain differences and to reject the notion that there is one specific ideal of being a human being whether it be a Platonic philosopher or a Heideggerian poet shepherding Being. In this chapter I explore Kristeva's claim that such a challenge to foundationalism is inherent to the psychoanalytic enterprise. I highlight how, despite her insistence on otherness, her theorizing of lesbian desire contains problematic contradictions which foreclose on the specificity and diversity of individuals' sexualities. I consider the relevance of Levinas's model of the face-to face relationship to analytic practices which are concerned with the uniqueness of each human being.

Understanding and the other

Many people come to analysis because they are locked within the Same, a totality of feeling, a way of being in the world that is uneasy, unbearable yet felt as irrevocable and fixed, not allowing for otherness. Is it the task of psychoanalysis to list these "fixations", label them as symptoms of known psychic conditions and prescribe the cure and thus to living both joy and vulnerability? This question highlights one central feature of psychoanalysis, namely, that it is not a practice of ontological topologies, not the practice of a question-answer structure within the parameters of thinking the truth of Being.

Within this ontological perspective there is an operative assumption that not only is the questioner involved in the Being that he questions but that Being is open to understanding. This leads to the view that, in principle, the enquirer is able to ground his own meaning through his relationship to Being. Here the question "who am I?" can be posed only as a "what-question" because Being can be approached only in terms of generality. This is exemplified by Gadamer's argument in *Truth and Method* that the primary hermeneutic requirement is one's own fore-understandings, as they are drawn from previous relations, to the matter in hand. This presence of anticipation and retention as text is an assertion that its formal structure not only expresses its *meanings* but also its *truth* (Gadamer, 1975, pp. 267–269). Here, then, the primary interpretation occurs in terms of a comprehension of the particular in the light of the general. The "I" as open to question, or as able to be understood, appears in the mode of generality. This means that the universal "I" is held in speech while its particularity escapes.

As Levinas argues, even if the question "who understands?" is answered by the monosyllabic "me", without any content, nonetheless, in this context the answer must mean "me who is known to you", "me whose voice you find in your memories", "me that you can situate in the system of your history". In this self-presencing of the Logos the "who" is lost in the articulation of "what". For Heidegger and Gadamer the answer to the question "who understands?" must take the form of an exposition of essence, for the question assumes that thinking and Being are within Being—the "who" is "one who understands". Thus, truth must consist in the exposition of Being to itself, in the consciousness of self, where consciousness implies knowledge or possession of self. This involves a denial of difference, of otherness, because it implies a sovereign thinker who reduces everything to himself through an intellectual grasp. An ontologist might object to this and argue that what escapes categorization is precisely the uniqueness of self and other; however, by describing the relationship with the other in terms of a totality or system which is completely open to understanding or interpretation the possibility is established of the relationship as able to be possessed by the one who understands, or interprets.

Freud's principal contribution to the twentieth century was the recognition of the resourceful character of the lived speech of one individual to another who then responds in a particular manner. What emerges from this conversation is, in a sense, a new speaking of that which is not anticipated, not already known, but yet is felt to be that which is most familiar. In the *Phaedo* (62b) Plato presented us with the notion of speech emergent from the inequality or asymmetry of interlocutors. Plato postulates the Stranger (*Phaedo,* 57b, 58b) as calling to the soul who dwells in her own place, alone. The role of the Stranger is such that he cannot be encompassed, yet by his call or invitation, he can highlight the presuppositions of the community. Desire emerges through the revelation of the other who calls to the autonomous subject and thereby destabilises the absoluteness of Being. Desire is not just an exigence towards immortality because its objective is the other, the Stranger: "The absolutely foreign alone can instruct us. And it is only man who could be absolutely foreign to me, refractory to every typology, to every genus, to every classification ..." (Levinas, 1961, p. 73).

Kristeva succinctly expresses the otherness inherent in the psychoanalytic enterprise:

> From past to present, from frustration to desire, from the parameter of pleasure to the parameter of death ... (the analyst) dazes the analysand with the unexpectedness of his interpretation: even so, however, the unexpectedness of the analysis is in any case sustained by a constant: the desire for the Other (1982b, p. 311).

In her paper "Psychoanalysis and the Polis" Kristeva discusses psychoanalytic interpretation which cannot be confined to a hermeneutics: the analyst does not give meaning or reassurance of identity to her patients, she does not speak from the position of a fixed system or prescriptive morality. Kristeva stresses the importance of the subject's symbolic integration of negativism, rejection, and the death drive, through his ability to distinguish propositional statements from speaking which is addressed to another for mutual understanding. The statement of a patient who says, "her eyes were wet", instead of telling the analyst that a woman he had seen was crying, is an example of a propositional statement.

Foundationalism and the search for origin

In Kristeva's view psychoanalysis challenges the foundationalism or formalism of western metaphysics. Such formalism involves shared notions of original experience and givenness. The experience is original, foundational, or ultimate because it is that to which all others refer, or to which they may be reduced, while it itself is not reducible to any other experience. Hence, whatever name is used—God, Being, History, Tradition—the origin, irreducible in its ultimateness, is both original as the ultimate experience and simultaneously originating as given origin. The positing of a foundational structure does not provide a model for pluralist expression, for the discourse of desires, wishes, fears. This involves an acknowledgement of asymmetry of human relationships, the difference yet relationship between speakers. The desire to possess one's own origin, to be one's self as self-knowledge, is the desire to exclude otherness or difference.

Kristeva argues that analytic speech reveals the desire to return to the origin, which she designates as the archaic mother. This desire subtends all speech. The archaic mother is resistant to meaning, she is unnameable. The task of the analyst is to open the space for the unnameable, to see it as a phantasm. This involves shifting obvious "realistic" meaning from speech to allow for the emergence of what Kristeva calls the meaninglessness or madness of desire. She maintains that one is ill when one is not loved. A central assumption of psychoanalysis is that present unhappiness, suffering, occurs because of failure of communication with others, primarily parents, in the past—the child speaks and is not heard; psychoanalysis then is communication about communication.

Central to this endeavour is the specification of subjectivity in terms of language and time. Against the Cartesian ego and Husserl's transcendental ego Kristeva specifies subjectivity as a process, the subject of enunciation. Philosophers are perennially questioning and reformulating the notion of time and subjectivity. Historians, archaeologists, physicists, biographers, religions, provide various theories of time in relation to the objects of their investigations. Psychoanalysis provides a theory of the genesis of the psyche—the timing of the subject in its instinctual and/or object relationships. Since three-month-old babies cannot speak in our syntax about their relationships, psychoanalysts have provided various hypotheses, in some cases claimed to be facts, based on their work with older people about the experiences of the early stages of life. Kristeva refers to this difficulty or impossibility of gaining access to childhood in *Desire in Language* and she maintains that in Western thought a discourse on childhood involves "a confrontation between thought and what it is not" (Kristeva, 1980, p. 276).

Subjects of enunciation

The Oedipus complex has been postulated in order to explain how it is that we become sex-gendered people and how we enter the symbolic order, language. Prior to this it is assumed that the baby functions with polymorphous instinctual drives and is established in a dyad with its mother. Kristeva's originality in this area is that by positing the subject as subject of enunciation she expands our notion of language to include the pre-Oedipal, pre-symbolic expression without subsuming it into the later syntactical development. She terms this early expression the semiotic relation:

> The *semiotic* (is) a psychosomatic modality of the signifying process; in other words, not a symbolic modality but one articulating (in the largest sense of the word) a continuum: the connections between the (glottal and anal) sphincters in (rhythmic and intonational) vocal modulations, or those between the sphincters and family protagonists, for example (Kristeva, 1984, pp. 28–29).

The semiotic is not simply a stage or phase surpassed in later integrations, but Kristeva emphasizes the fact that the subject is always both semiotic and symbolic. She uses the Platonic term, *chora*, to elucidate the various processes anterior to sign and syntax. The notion of the chora also helps us to consider the genesis of psychic pain, suffering, sadness. Kristeva specifies the chora as the place where the subject is both generated and negated, where the unity of the subject is fragmented by the changes and stases that produce him. Although the chora is not a "meaning" available to representation it is, nevertheless, a modality of significance "in which the linguistic sign is not yet articulated as the absence of an object and as the distinction of real and symbolic" (Kristeva, 1984, p. 26). Kristeva specifies the symbolic as arising from the relation to the other through constraints of biological differences and historical family structures. The symbolic stage of development begins with the mirror stage to which psychoanalysts have attributed the capacities for absence and representation.

The unnameable: phobia, narcissism, borderline psychosis?

As I have already mentioned, Kristeva stresses the importance of the subject's desire to return to the resistant archaic mother and the way in which the analyst's attentiveness to the desire opens space for the unnameable. In *Powers of Horror* Kristeva offers a fascinating analysis of borderline psychosis in the context of the pre-oedipal relationship of the baby to its mother, focussing on feelings of rejection, fear, and aggression. The term "abjection" is introduced in order to describe the revulsion and horror of the pre-oedipal attempt to separate from the mother, that is, the attempt to separate from the mother prior to the autonomy of language: "The abject is the violence of mourning for an 'object' that has always already been lost" (Kristeva, 1982, p. 15). Kristeva posits abjection as the object of primary repression. Abjection shatters narcissism when repression is released and the "the death that I am provokes horror" (Kristeva, 1982, p. 25).

In a commentary on "Little Hans" Kristeva elaborates the kind of communication that is effected by phobic states. Processes of condensation are integral to the production of phobias. The phobic "object" is not an already constituted object but rather the representative of drive. Communication through phobias arises from an incapacity to produce metaphors. In this context analysis has two main tasks, first, the restitution of a memory, a language, to unnameable and nameable states of fear, and second, to make the analysand aware of the void underpinning the play with the signifier and primary processes. Kristeva describes the language of phobia as one of "want" (Kristeva, 1982, pp. 34–38). Here language itself has become a counter-phobic object, it barricades a discourse which has to be tracked down through that which is not spoken.

Margaret Little, the eminent British Object Relations psychoanalyst designates borderline psychosis as a state of undifferentiation between the psyche and *soma* and the failure of fusion between ego and id. States of excitement are felt as threats of annihilation. Kristeva develops this position by describing this state of being in the world in terms of experiencing a collapse of a border between one's body and the world. Here one is flooded with bodily insides—the fluidity of blood, sperm, excrement. She describes the abjection of these flows which become the sole object of sexual desire. The subject of borderline psychosis, like any speaker, fears castration but for him it is not only a part of himself that he loses but his whole life. His immersion in the bodily flow spares him the risk of a castration which is integral to a relationship with an other. Kristeva maintains that the borderline subject is asking for a rebirth in which he can find the speech that belongs to him. She argues that the borderline patient has never felt loved for himself because, paradoxically, his mother loved only him, she did not love any other: "The oedipal negation of the father is here linked with a complaint against an adhesive maternal wrapping and it leads the subject towards psychic pain dominated by the inability to love" (Kristeva, 1983, p. 251).

During psychoanalytic treatment the borderline subject identifies with the analyst. Kristeva specifies two types of identification, first, a primal one resulting from affection for the archaic mother as well as anxious guilt, and second, the introjection into the ego of an object that is already libidinal. Kristeva argues that the borderline subject exists only insofar as he identifies with the other insofar as the other speaks. The analyst while being the object of identification is also a non-object in that he evokes the analysand's non-object-orientated layers of drives. This allows for the possibility of transference with people in non-object-orientated psychic states such as a borderline state.

Kristeva traces the genesis of archaic unity in terms of the phallus desired by the mother. The identity of the mother and her desire is the phallic unity of the imaginary father. Kristeva argues that primary identification involves a transference to/from the imaginary father and that this is correlative with the mother being abjected: "Narcissism would be that correlation (with the imaginary father and the abjected mother) enacted around the central empti-ness of that transference" (Kristeva, 1983, p. 257). Narcissism is a defence against the emptiness of separation and the representations, projections, identifications involved in it are attempts to deny that emptiness. Psychosis reveals that the representation of our speech rests upon emptiness. Kristeva warns of the analytic danger of con-ceiving narcissism as origin as unanalysable. This can result in the presentation of interpretative discourse as either comfortably reas-suring or as a confrontational hostility; these attitudes on the part of the analyst collude with the narcissistic state. This is why Kristeva stresses the importance of opening out the more archaic operations of the psyche.

Face-to-face with differences

Kristeva praises Freud for challenging the western concept of sub-jectivity in terms of self-conscious rationality. The notion of the unconscious introduces otherness and dethrones the epistemologi-cal primacy of the ego. The question of difference, heterogeneity, arises within a discussion of what is sometimes interpreted as the solipsistic formulation offered by psychoanalysis. A common argu-ment proposed against psychoanalysis is the self-justification of its theoretical stand; disagreements are interpreted in terms of repres-sion and defence. Can the analysand say "no" to the analyst's inter-pretation without this being interpreted as a defence? It depends on the specific situation whether the "no" is in fact operating as a defence or whether it is an assertion of separateness. Can one assert this and remain in analysis? Is every exchange within the analytic situation a matter of transference and counter-transference interpretable, at least in principle, by the analyst? If this "no" is not transferential yet acknowledged, what then is the status of the interlocutors—do they remain analyst and analysand or is this a collapse into a humanistic conception of an exchange between two self-contained egos?

In his "Letter on Humanism" Heidegger argues that all forms of humanism agree that the humanity of man is already determined with regard to an already established interpretation of nature, history and the world. Furthermore, language becomes a tool, a means of communication which is determined by the public realm which decides in advance what is intelligible and what must be rejected as unintelligible. A humanistic specification of the interlocutors would, then, preclude otherness, difference. In a culture dominated by the *logos* there is no fundamental interruption, for all contestation and interruption of discourse is automatically translated in terms of the discourse itself. Hence, as Gadamer argues, it survives the death of the interlocutors who utter it as cultural heritage assuring the very continuity of the culture itself.

Levinas (1961) introduces his notion of the asymmetry of human relationships in terms of the face-to-face relation. Here the Other in his otherness cannot appear as the result of an objectifying act, that is, in the affirmation that the object of consciousness, while distinct from consciousness, is a production of consciousness (See Levinas, 1974b). Levinas (1961) proposes the model of the face-to-face relationship in order to designate the irreplaceable uniqueness of each human being where this uniqueness is precisely what escapes categorization. He argues that it is in relationship to the other person/ persons that this arises. What is at issue is the specification of subjectivity as ethical, that is, as separate, other, yet in a relationship of responsibility, vulnerability. The subjects are specified as interlocutors, each inviting the other to respond, to move out of egocentricity, yet where this response is not "meaningful", it is "for nothing". Otherness here is specified as that which cannot be thematized yet is the specificity of an individual in relation to me.

The realm beyond intentionality, as communication, introduces otherness not as the term of a project, but as the relation with the neighbour in the sense of he who has meaning before one gives it to him. The face is not a presence announcing an "unsaid" which lies behind and which, in principle, could be said. The face-to-face is a saying that in being said at each moment breaks the definition of that which it says, and breaks through the totality that it embraces. Levinas's task is not one of distinguishing between the lived, as spontaneously operative, and efforts to account for it critically as operative totality. Even within the confines of a more traditional kind of phenomenological investigation the notion of lived experience is not treated merely as simple repetition of that which has already gone before. The work of Gadamer and Merleau-Ponty, for example, stresses that questions can be asked which challenge and which seek to overcome the insights held in our cultural store. But Levinas's central point here is that responsibility of one-for-the-Other does not occur within the tension of a naïve, lived, unreflection which would be available to thematization in some manner. For the interval, or difference, which separates one from the Other, as well as the non-difference of the one-for-the-Other cannot be simply gathered into a theme, or established as a state of the soul (Levinas, 1967, p. 232).

Psychoanalysis and sexual difference: Contradictions

Kristeva claims that it is psychoanalysis that gives heterogeneity an analysable status by designating it as sexual desire and/or death wish. She interprets deconstruction as relativizing truth and thereby not adequate for theorizing the analytic process which she maintains is centrally concerned with truth (of interpretation) and the ethical. For her a practice is ethical when it dissolves narcissistic fixations "to which the signifying process succumbs in its socio-symbolic realization" (Kristeva, 1984, p. 233).

What is the ethical stand of psychoanalysis *vis-à-vis* its claim to account for sexual difference? In "Stabat Mater" Kristeva stresses the irreconcilable interest in both sexes in asserting their differences. To what extent does psychoanalysis allow for the unveiling of this interest? In pursuing the question of how we become men and women, of explaining heterosexuality, is there some operative assumption that we know about homosexuality, that we can explain adult desire in terms of regression or fixation? Can desire be an object of explanation? How can psychoanalysis reconcile its claim to acknowledge the specificity of each person's love and fear while its theoretical stand maintains expressions such as the following from Kristeva:

> Beneath homosexual libido, which our social objectives catch and maintain captive, the chasms of narcissistic emptiness spread out; although the latter can be a powerful motive for ideal or supergotic cathexis, it is also the primary source of inhibition (Kristeva, 1983, p. 258).

and

> ... the girl ... will retain the traces of that primary transference only if assisted by a father having a maternal character, who nevertheless will not be of much help in her breaking away from the mother and finding a heterosexual object. She will thus tend to bury that primal identification under the disappointed feverishness of the homosexual, or else in abstraction which, as it flies away from the body, fully constitute itself as 'soul' or fuses with an Idea, a Love, a Self-Sacrifice (Kristeva, 1983, p. 262).

How can psychoanalysis think sexual difference if it works with an operative assumption of "knowing" sexuality, exemplified in many cases by the refusal, until comparatively recently, of major psychoanalytic institutes to accept lesbians and homosexual men as training candidates? (See Ellis, 1994).

I have argued that it is of crucial importance that there is consistency between the practical claims made by psychotherapists and their "theoretical" claims, that is, concern for the status of their ontological, epistemological, and, most important, ethical statements. I have introduced some concepts of central importance in Kristeva's elaboration of psychoanalytical notions of time, language, and subjectivity. Finally, I have questioned the consistency of her position on the interpretation of the central issue of psychoanalysis, that of sexual desire. Psychoanalysts devote a lot of attention to elucidating the difficulty of separating from the mother. My question is, why is it that psychoanalysts have such difficulty in separating from the Father?

CHAPTER FIVE

Shifting the ego towards a body subject

Mary Lynne Ellis

In this chapter I consider Freud's notion of the ego in the light of other theories of subjectivity within the field of continental philosophy, namely those of Foucault and Merleau-Ponty. The work of most British-trained analysts, with the exception of those trained in the Lacanian or Jungian schools, continues to be underpinned by a notion of subjectivity in which the concept of the ego is central. In this view of subjectivity it is assumed that human beings live in a perpetual state of conflict between the id's passionate drives and the regulating function of the ego. My aim here is to consider the limitations of this view of subjectivity in theory and practice. Although there have been a number of challenges to Freud's theorising of the ego by, for example, the Object Relations schools these have tended to revolve around questions as to when, developmentally, the ego is formed and as to whether or not "ego strength" should be the goal of psychoanalysis. Such theorising does not extend to a more fundamental questioning as to the values informing this conceptualisation of subjectivity and how far the notion of the "ego" is crucial to the practice of psychoanalysis.

Questions regarding how we conceptualise the ego are not abstract; they matter to clinical practice because our particular notions of maturity and of "healthy" relationships underpin our responses to our patients consciously and unconsciously. Our formulations arise from a particular cultural and historical context and arise from within a specific tradition of Western philosophical thought. If we adhere uncritically to this tradition how can we be sufficiently sensitive to the uniqueness and diversity of our patients" experiences, particularly those of people who are not from white Western backgrounds? In presenting a critical consideration of Freud's (1923b) formulation of the ego in *The Ego and the Id*, my aim is to highlight the importance of a conceptualisation of subjectivity which acknowledges the social and cultural specificity of people's experiences.

Too often such an approach to subjectivity is dismissed by analysts: they claim that the complexity of the individual is being lost, and that the "truth" of the individual resides in the depth of an "internal" world, which is separate and distinct from the socio-cultural context. However, for those of us who work with people from a diversity of class and cultural backgrounds and with people from a range of sexual orientations, it is increasingly apparent that to disregard the social context is to be profoundly neglectful of an individual's specific experience of their own subjectivity as it appears in wishes, dreams, and fantasies. Furthermore, it is not sufficient to merely "add on" a recognition of political and social context; how a person speaks to us in psychotherapy of their suffering and their joy, their anger and their passion is shaped and produced by the cultural context. If we do not acknowledge this we fail to recognise the complexity and richness of their struggles and conflicts.

Freud's (1923b) notion of the ego in *The Ego and the Id* deserves close attention since his conceptualisations, as the first pioneer of psychoanalysis, continue to influence how the ego is understood by most analysts contemporaneously. Although Freud had the courage to constantly question and revise his theories, his tone is that of an acultural "objectivity". For example, he claims that his description of the ego arises from "various facts of analytic observation" (Freud, 1923b, p. 12). However, as I shall argue, the ego is, on the contrary, a culturally specific concept, which is underpinned by various intellectual traditions and socio-cultural values which Freud does not acknowledge. An examination of the concept of the ego thus offers the possibility for analysts and social scientists to consider how our theorising and practice are themselves shaped by particular values and, furthermore, to consider the limitations of a psychoanalytic theorising and practice which do not address the social context of the individual.

I will demonstrate how Freud's claims of "objectivity" arise from the influence of Enlightenment philosophers and their view that "science" can offer us certain knowledge about the world. I shall argue that his association of the ego with "reason" and "science" does not sufficiently allow for the impact of the social context on the constitution of subjectivity (Freud, 1923b, p. 25). In contrast, Foucault's account of power as *producing* bodies and sexualities can enable psychoanalysts to be more sensitive to the multiple meanings of for example, sexuality and aggression (Foucault, 1984, p. 105). Freud's account is also restricted by the dualistic thinking characteristic of the Cartesian tradition. (Descartes, 1968, pp. 156–157). This is highlighted particularly in his account of the gendered ego where the binary oppositions of "masculinity" and "femininity" do not allow for the socio-cultural specificity of these terms. (Freud, 1923b, pp. 31–33). Moreover, his claim that the Oedipus complex, which is central in his theorising of the ego, is universal does not allow for the diversity of sexualities and their socio-historical specificity. As Franz Fanon (1986, p. 152) and Bronislaw Malinowski (in Jones, 1928, p. 365) argue, the Oedipus complex assumes Western European patterns of familial organisation. I shall argue that Freud's notion of the ego does not sufficiently allow for cultural diversity.

In contrast to Freud's account of the ego, Merleau-Ponty theorises subjectivity as culturally and historically specific (Merleau-Ponty, 1962, p. 189). His subject is a "body subject", "intentional" and embodied, oriented towards the world and he challenges the dichotomies of "internal" and "external" which are operative in Freud's account. I shall argue that Merleau-Ponty's view of subjectivity can contribute to the development of a psychoanalytic approach which is truly sensitive and alive to difference and diversity.

The mechanics of the reasonable ego

Freud's failure to acknowledge that his observations are informed by a number of assumptions, which arise from his specific cultural and historical position is evident throughout *The Ego and the Id*. (Freud, 1923b, pp. 12–66) For example, he writes "these thoughts are linked to various *facts* of analytic observation" (my italics) (Freud, 1923b, p. 12). He describes the ego as an observable "entity" (Freud, 1923b, p. 23). In claiming that he is writing from a position of neutrality, that of objectivity, he does not acknowledge that "objectivity" is itself culturally determined. Freud's assumption that there are objective, universal standards through which truth can be determined is in line with Enlightenment thinking. The Enlightenment was an intellectual movement which began in England in the 17th century and developed in France and Germany in the 18th century. It is informed by a view of man as rational by nature. Enlightenment philosophers view reason as crucial to the acquisition of knowledge and privilege "science" as the ideal form of knowledge. The use of reason enables "man" to think and act correctly, and reason is claimed by Enlightenment thinkers to be ahistorical and acultural. This view of human subjectivity continued to influence Western philosophical and popular thought in Freud's time.

Freud's theorising of the ego reflects the Enlightenment's view of subjectivity. He claims that the passions of the id, which are ruled by the desire for pleasure (the "pleasure principle") are brought under control by the ego. Although Freud refers to the ego as part of the id, he simultaneously emphasises their distinctness, claiming "the ego represents what may be called reason and common sense, in contrast to the id, which contains the passions." (Freud, 1923b, p. 25). He describes the relation between the ego and the id as analogous to that between a rider and his horse. The rider has to control the superior power of the horse, although, in order not to be parted from his horse, he also at times has to guide the horse in the direction it wants to go. Similarly, the ego has to respond to the demands of the id as they were its own.

In line with the Enlightenment's privileging of science, Freud also draws on analogies from anatomy and science. Fromm argues that Freud's theorising was particularly influenced by the work of von Brucke, a physiologist and specialist in mechanistic materialism who had taught him (Fromm, 1978, p. 48). Mechanistic materialism was based on the principle that all psychic processes can be explained and understood through a knowledge of physiological processes. The effects of this view are evident in the anatomical analogies, which run through Freud's account in *The Ego and the Id*. For example, Freud describes the ego as wearing a "cap of hearing" (Freud, 1923b, p. 25), the perceptual system forming its surface "more or less as the germinal disc rests upon the ovum" (Freud, 1923b, p. 24). It is a part of a "mental apparatus" in which unpleasurable sensations and feelings "exert a driving force" and seek "discharge", enabling a lessening of tension (Freud, 1923b, p. 22). The ego "secures a postponement of motor discharges and controls the access to motililty" (Freud, 1923b, p. 55). Even where Freud introduces these descriptions as analogies the effect he conveys is that the ego and its workings are as tangible as a part of the body, a piece of the brain, rather than concepts.

Although Freud attended the seminars of the philosopher Brentano in the 1890s, he does not acknowledge the impact of Western philosophical thought on his theorising. Instead, he gathers support for this view of the human subject as torn between reason and passion from the popular view of his time: "All this falls in line with popular distinctions which we are all familiar with" (Freud, 1923b, p. 25). He thus takes the popular distinction between reason and passion as evidence of its truth rather than as a truth designated as such by the dominant discourse of the time.

The notion of a rational subject as an ahistorical, acultural subject in Enlightenment thought has been criticised by a number of European philosophers, including Heidegger, Merleau-Ponty, and Foucault. They question the notion of universal, rational, and objective standards by which goodness or truth can be determined. In their view what constitutes "reason" is itself always historically and culturally specific and would also challenge the notion of "passions" as a-lingustic and acultural. They argue for a notion of subjectivity as always shifting and contextual, historically and culturally, never fixed.

As analysts working with people from a diversity of social backgrounds, including race and class, a view of subjectivity as contextual can enable allow us to be open to more complex understandings of the specific shifting and interwoven positions taken up by our patients in different social contexts. In adhering to Freud's Enlightenment view of what constitutes a "mature" ego we risk being insensitive to their particular uniqueness and differences. In the case example at the end of the chapter I will demonstrate in more detail the crucial importance of a view of subjectivity as shifting and socially and culturally specific to our clinical practice.

It could be argued that Freud's radical claims with regard to the disruptive effects of the unconscious challenge the Enlightenment view of the subject. In *The Ego and the Id* he simultaneously conveys the ego as a "monarch" *and* a "submissive slave who courts his master's love" (Freud, 1923b, p. 56). The ego is a slave to its master, the id, because its methods of taking control of the id involve disguising its conflicts with reality. Furthermore, in attaching the id's libido to itself (through identification) it assists the death instincts in the id to gain control over the libido. In so doing, it runs the risk of becoming the object of the death instincts and being destroyed. It is at risk too of the super-ego's harsh demands. The ego is thus described by Freud as "the actual seat of anxiety" (Freud, 1923b, p. 57). This strand in Freud's account appears to challenge the notion of the rational subject of the Enlightenment. However, he does not go far enough. He argues that, ultimately, the goal of analysis is "to enable the ego to achieve a progressive conquest of the id" (Freud, 1923b, p. 56).

Words and drives

Freud argues that there is a distinction between unconscious sensations or feelings and unconscious ideas. This reflects his assumption, derived from his understanding of scientific explanations, that there is an observable world, which lies beyond language and interpretation. He argues that unconscious ideas rely on a connection to "word-presentations", residues of memories, which are derived from the preconscious (Freud, 1923b, p. 20) whereas feelings are either conscious or unconscious and do not depend on transmission through "word-presentations" even if they are connected with them. This distinction between unconscious feelings and sensations and unconscious ideas arises from an assumption by Freud that there is an extra-linguistic, a-cultural, natural world of drives or instincts which arise within us which are then negotiated by the ego and the super-ego, subject to various defences such as resistance and repression. One of these drives is "the uninhibited sexual instinct proper" (Freud, 1923b, p. 40).

This view of language was being challenged by philosophers contemporaneous with Freud, such as Heidegger. For Heidegger, language is not a communication from the interior of one subject to the interior of another; instead, speaking occurs within a background of already shared meanings particular to a given linguistic community. Language is therefore always contextual; it is not the "external" expression of something "inner":

> In telling, Dasein *expresses* itself not because it has, in the first instance, been encapsulated as something "internal" over against something outside, but because as Being-in-the-world it is already "outside" when it understands. What is expressed is precisely this Being-outside (Heidegger, 1962, p. 205).

The view we take on language and subjectivity is crucial to analytic practice. For example, if we accept Freud's view that unconscious, a-cultural impulses become socialised through the control of the ego and the super-ego, through restriction and prohibition, we assume that there are natural impulses that can be known and universally identified as, for example, sexual or aggressive. How can we "know" these except through the medium of language, whether spoken or visual? The inseparability of feelings and language is highlighted by Merleau-Ponty, the French philosopher, a phenomenologist and a major, although little acknowledged, influence on Foucault:

> It would be legitimate to speak of "natural signs" only if the anatomical organization of our body produced a correspond-ence between specific gestures and given "states of mind". The fact is that the behaviour associated with anger or love is not the same in a Japanese and an Occidental (person). Or, to be more precise, the difference of behaviour corresponds to a difference in the emotions themselves (Merleau-Ponty, 1962, pp. 188–189).

For Merleau-Ponty there are no natural, a-cultural and a-linguistic impulses as Freud theorises. His emphasis on the specificity of language, whether verbal or non-verbal, is important for practising psychotherapists. Our medium is language yet there are few debates in the mainstream psychoanalytic world regarding the theories of language, which inform our work. Merleau-Ponty's theorising high-lights the importance for psychotherapists of an acute sensitivity to the specific words and gestures of our patients. Furthermore, it emphasises the dangers of assuming that there are thoughts and feelings that we can "know" and identify "scientifically" as anger and aggression. If we are committed to a practice which is sensitive to cultural differences it is crucial to understand, as Merleau-Ponty argues, that such thoughts and feelings are experienced and expressed in an enormous diversity of ways, depending on the particular cultural context.

Foucault takes Merleau-Ponty's theorising further by arguing that, in any particular culture, certain discourses become dominant and shape our interpretations of the world. He argues against Freud's notion of repression, claiming that discourses *produce* sexuality in such a form that it comes to appear as natural: there are no "natural" sexual instincts outside discourse which then undergo repression. By this he means that interpretations of the body and sexuality as natural unities are the *effects* of discourses. For Foucault there is no body, which is factually distinct prior to history or discourse. In being "totally imprinted" by history the body is saturated with and moreover, *produced* by historical forces (Foucault, 1984, p. 148).

The ego, the super-ego and power

Foucault's critique may be better understood if we compare his understanding of the operations of power within our culture with Freud's notion of the super-ego on which his formulation depends. The super-ego is a part of the ego which can also stand apart from the ego. It manifests itself as a sense of guilt since it is associated with a prohibitive, morally judgemental and harshly critical (voice) derived primarily from the child's identification with the power of its father who, for Freud, holds the main seat of authority. Cultural prohibitions have a secondary influence in shaping the super-ego. The ego is constantly involved in a battle for control over the demands of the id, the natural feelings and sensations arising unconsciously from within the individual's body, while also being under threat of the restraints of the super-ego. According to Lear (1998) Freud's tripartheid structure of the psyche is derived from Plato. Plato's conception of the psyche had three parts: appetite (for food and sex), "spirit" (concerned with pride, honour and anger), and reason (which seeks knowledge).

Freud's conception of how power operates is highlighted in his description of the ego's relation to the id as analogous with a rider trying to control his horse and also that of a "constitutional monarch" poised to impose his veto on any proposed parliamentary measure (Freud, 1923b, p. 55). This view of power as imposed from above contrasts with Foucault's view that power is not only prohibitive, it is also productive. For example, in his description of how religious confession required the admission of forbidden sexual thoughts and practices he argues that this paradoxically led to a proliferation of discourses on sex and sexual practices: "Power operated as a mechanism of attraction, it drew out those peculiarities over which it kept watch ... power anchored the pleasure it uncovered" (Foucault, 1978, p. 45). The power that scrutinises sexualities for the purposes of restriction is thus simultaneously involved in their production.

Foucault's theorising with regard to power and subjectivity offers a solution to the problem often posed by analysts as to the relation between the "internal" worlds of their patients and the "external" world, namely the wider socio-political context. This problem arises from the presupposition of a clear division between these two worlds, which as I will argue in the next section of the chapter, arises from the Cartesian heritage that structured much of Freud's thinking. Foucault's theorising of how subjectivities and sexualities are themselves formed through the convergence of multiple, shifting discourses which arise at a particular historical time and within a particular cultural context cuts across what are regarded as fundamental oppositional distinctions. These oppositions, Foucault argues, are effects of dominant discourses; they do not exist prior to these discourses. His theorising highlights for psychoanalysts that our understanding of the broader socio-cultural and historical contexts of our patients cannot be simply "added on" to our interpretations of our patients' unconscious and internal worlds. Subjectivity is itself produced through and by the social context with its specific constellations of social and familial relations and childrearing practices.

Cartesian dualisms

The influence of Descartes (1596–1650) can be discerned throughout Freud's account of the ego and its workings. His theorising is premised on dualistic distinctions between reason and passion, thinking and feeling, culture and nature, mind and body, internal and external. These dualisms originate from Descartes' conception of the world as being divided into two distinct entities, matter and mind or spirit (these two are not differentiated). He defined matter as spatial, extended and divisible and mind as non-spatial, unextended and indivisible. Although, according to Descartes, these are entirely different substances, they are nevertheless co-joined, a paradox which is not addressed by him (see Cottingham, 1995, p. 191).

Freud's conceptualisation of the ego as having both conscious and unconscious aspects (Freud, 1923b, p. 17) appears to throw into question many of the dualisms which Freud's theorising generally relies on. Although the ego is unconscious, it is not repressed. However, just as repressed unconscious contents do, it exerts powerful effects and requires analytic work in order for it to become conscious. Drawing on the psychoanalyst Groddeck Freud develops this formulation further by proposing that the "entity" which is modified by the perceptual system and begins by being pre-conscious, is the ego (Freud, 1923b, p. 23). The ego extends into the "id" (also Groddeck's term): the ego is therefore "that part of the id which has been modified by the direct influence of the external world" (Freud, 1923b, p. 25). In this section of *The Ego and the Id*, binary oppositional distinctions between conscious and unconscious, ego and id, internal and external, begin to dissolve. However, this leads Freud to a radical question from which he takes flight: "When we find ourselves thus confronted by the necessity of postulating a third *Ucs.*, which is not repressed, we must admit that the characteristic of being unconscious begins to lose significance for us" (Freud, 1923b, p. 18). The question appears to raise too much of a challenge because, as he admits, "the property of being conscious or not is in the last resort our one beacon-light in the darkness of depth-psychology" (Freud, 1923b, p. 18).

Freud thus returns to the safety of the Cartesian tradition. His distinctions between the "unconscious feelings" and "drives", which arise from *within* an individual's body, and the external world, requiring the mediation of the ego (Freud, 1923b, p. 25), between "unconscious feelings" and "unconscious ideas" or "thoughts" (Freud 1923b, p. 20), and between the ego as "reason" as opposed to the id with its unruly "passions" (Freud, 1971, p. 25) all echo Descartes" dualisms. Freud's classification of unconscious drives into opposing categories of life (Eros) and death instincts in *Beyond the Pleasure Principle* (Freud, 1920, pp. 52–60) and further developed in *The Ego and the Id* (Freud, 1923b, pp. 40–47) also presupposes such dualisms. In both these accounts Freud is explicit about his "fundamental dualistic point of view", emphasising "we cannot escape that view" (Freud, 1923b, p. 46).

Descartes' view that opposing substances and forces exist objectively in themselves does not take into account the effects of language in our interpretation of the world. He assumes that there is an objective world composed of two substances which we then name through language. From a Foucauldian point of view, the binary oppositions of Descartes have continued to operate as a dominant discourse arising from a particular intellectual tradition in the West. They do not name an already existing state of things; they instead "produce" this view of the world (Foucault, 1978, p. 105).

Freud is unaware that Cartesian dualistic thinking *informs* his clinical observations (which he assumes are value-free) and arises from a particular cultural and linguistic tradition. This leads him to establish false problems and speculative solutions. For example, in presupposing a sharp polarity between love and hate, Freud is forced to solve the question as to how we can account for cases in which it appears that one of them is transformed into the other without relinquishing his prior assumption. A circuitous theorising is required to account for this, leading to the development of concepts such as "sublimation" and "desexualised ego-libido" (Freud, 1923b, pp. 45–46). These in turn become established as if they are objectively observable entities or processes.

The consequences of this are highly relevant to analytic practice. If we uncritically assume that there are oppositional entities and processes which lie outside language, we are unlikely to be sufficiently attentive to the unique, shifting, and particular relations between the conscious and unconscious aspects of our patients' experiences which are always already within language, whether visual or verbal. Indeed, for many patients, the rigid oppositionality of many of their distinctions is a major source of their distress. As the analytic work develops, these dualisms become less acute and possibilities for more flexible and subtle distinctions emerge.

The gendered ego

Freud's account of the gendering of the ego further reflects his dualistic thinking. He argues in *The Ego and the Id* that the ego is in danger of pathology if its identifications are "too numerous, unduly powerful and incompatible with one another" (Freud, 1923b, p. 30). Although Freud's account allows for a shifting and somewhat precarious path *towards* "masculinity" and "femininity", he is highly prescriptive regarding the final identification, which constitutes the achievement of the "mature" ego's masculinity or femininity. The Oedipus complex is pivotal in the negotiation of gender identifications and, for Freud, it is universal: "every new arrival on this planet is faced with the task of mastering the Oedipus complex" (Freud, 1905d, p. 226). In the case of the boy, the threat of castration forces him to relinquish the object-cathexis of his mother and either identify with her or intensify his identification with his father. Freud is explicit as to which outcome is more "normal", namely the latter identification: "In this way the dissolution of the Oedipus complex would consolidate the masculinity in a boy's character" (Freud, 1923b, p. 32). For girls, the "normal" outcome is identification with her mother. This will, according to Freud "fix the child's feminine character" (Freud, 1923b, p. 32). For both sexes, the super-ego has a specifically masculine character, that of the father.

Freud acknowledges that there is a contradiction in his view of how masculine and feminine identifications occur (Freud, 1923b, p. 32). His first assumption is that the ego is constituted by identifications with lost objects and it thus "contains the history of those object choices" (Freud, 1923b, p. 29). Since Freud assumes that the child's passion at the Oedipal stage is for the parent of the opposite sex, which subsequently has to be relinquished, it could be assumed that its ego identification would be with that lost parental object. Yet in his account of the dissolution of the Oedipus complex, normal resolution involves identification with the parent of the same sex. This is not consistent with his notion that identification is predicated on loss. Interestingly, he argues that it is more common for a girl to take up the abandoned object into her ego, identifying with her father but, he claims, this outcome depends on "the masculinity in her disposition" (Freud, 1923b, p. 32).

Thus the gendering of the ego ultimately depends more on biology than on social or historical factors. Furthermore, he does not allow for the historical and cultural specificity of terms such as "masculinity" and "femininity". He associates femininity with passivity, a weak super-ego, and sexual desire for men. Masculinity is diametrically opposed to this, reflecting the dualistic thinking which pervades Freud's thought; it is associated with activity and aggression, a strong super-ego, and sexual desire for women.

In his introduction of the notion of a "complete Oedipus complex" (Freud, 1923b, p. 33), Freud appears to be proffering a more complex account of gender identification. It arises from the bisexuality he considers originally present in children and subsequent ambivalent relations to the parents. In this scenario the boy, for example, has an ambivalent relation to his father and an affectionate relation to his mother and, simultaneously, "behaves like a girl" in an affectionate relation to his father and in a hostile rivalry in relation to his mother (Freud, 1923b, p. 33). This account, while adhering to normative notions of "masculinity" and "femininity" allows for more diversity and does not seem to presuppose a dominance or fixity within either gender. However, Freud goes on to elaborate how the existence of this "complete Oedipus complex" is to be found in neurotics (Freud, 1923b, p. 33). The dissolution of the complex will result in a mother-identification and a father-identification within the ego but "the relative intensity of the two identifications in any individual will reflect the preponderance in him of one or other of the two sexual dispositions" (Freud, 1923b, p. 34). Freud again resorts to a biological determinism in his theorising of the gendered ego.

Freud assumes that "normal" sexual development for men and women results in heterosexuality. For example, in *The Ego and the Id*, he associates homosexuality in men with the transformation of an aggressive hostile attitude into an affectionate object-choice (Freud, 1923b, pp. 37, 43). Although he makes a radical claim for his time that there is an original bisexuality in babies and young children, prior to the negotiation of the Oedipus complex, he nevertheless assumes that normal resolution of this leads to heterosexuality.

(See O'Connor & Ryan, 1993, for a thorough critique of the Oedipus complex in relation to the theorizing of lesbian sexuality).

Freud's accounts of the vicissitudes of the path of the libido from the bisexuality of infancy, through the Oedipus complex and arriving finally at a masculine or feminine identification with a heterosexual orientation is inconsistent since it is interwoven with a number of different and often contradictory discourses. His assumption of an original bisexuality implies a bisexuality, which is already biologically given. However, the child's libido is then shaped through its social relations with its parents. Freud fails to see that these familial relations are situated within a wider context. For example, his assumption that the child's first love object in the "pre-Oedipal" stage is the biological birthmother (as opposed to the father or other carers) reflects a biologistic view which does not take into account the wider social context and patterns of child care specific to early twentieth century Europe. The next stage, the Oedipal, involves complex struggles for the child with its desires for the parent of the opposite sex. This involves a momentous switch of affection for the girl, which Freud explains through the notion of penis envy. The girl's envy for the penis as superior organ leads her to desire her father, thus precipitating her Oedipus complex. Again, there is a shift into biologism as well as a presumption of inferiority in girls and women: the girl does not, biologically have a penis and, it is assumed, she cannot help perceiving this as a lack. This "lack" catapults her into a particular relation with her father, which Freud assumes is one of desire. His notion of penis envy arises out of a prior normative assumption that girls and boys have to have a heterosexual attraction to one of their parents and the necessity of explaining how this occurs in girls. Finally, however, identification with the parent of the same sex and taking up a masculine position as a boy and a feminine position as a girl depends on "sexual disposition". Where does this sexual disposition arise from if children are, as Freud also claims, originally bisexual? Freud begins and ends with a biological given in his account of "normal" development, although these "givens" appear to contradict one another.

In Freud's account of the gendering of the ego it is evident that he is limited by the Enlightenment view of subjectivity and its commitment to "science" as the ideal form of knowledge. This cuts across the more radical possibilities of his theorising of bisexual possibilities and the precarious identifications taken up by the ego. "Masculinity" and "femininity" are achieved as final states of maturity, held as universal for men and for women. Freud's conceptions of masculinity and femininity have been the target of a number of feminist critiques. (See, for example, Chodorow, 1978; Eichenbaum & Orbach, 1982; Irigaray, 1985 and O'Connor & Ryan, 1993). Many of them have focussed on the particular restrictions that Freud's view of the mature "feminine" ego have placed on women and argued that this arose from the particular socio-historical context in which Freud practised, namely a middle class patriarchal European culture of the first quarter of the twentieth century. It is crucial that analysts critically consider the assumptions which, underpinned Freud's theorising at that time and also examine how far these continue to inform their own views of "maturity" in both men and women. It is also important to acknowledge the current socio-historical factors which shape our own critiques and developments in our own theorising. Such questioning has major implications for clinical analytic work. If analysts fail to consider them, they are unlikely to be sufficiently open to the multiplicity of interpretations of masculinity and femininity brought by their patients, some of which may be restrictive and some productive, according to the unique experience of each individual patient.

The economic ego

Freud's conceptions of familial organisation and of "masculinity" and "femininity" arise from a specific context, namely middle-class Vienna in the first quarter of the nineteenth century. Fromm argues that it is crucial to consider how far this economic context shaped Freud's conceptualisation of the libido. (Fromm, 1978, p. 51). He describes the ethos of European middle class businessmen, amongst whom Freud practised, as based on a principle of scarcity and on the value of saving. According to Fromm, Freud's concept of libidinal impulses seeking discharge with the aim of easing unpleasurable tensions reflect this principle. In a context in which commodities are limited, Freud's notion of desire is thus founded on lack, rather than on abundance.

The assumption that desire arises from lack has been challenged by the feminist philosopher, Grosz, who argues for a conceptualisation of desire as *productive,* occurring between skin surfaces rather than arising from those zones designated by Freud as specifically erotogenic. She conceptualises desire in terms of "proliferation" and "intensifications" which strongly contrast with those of lack and scarcity (Grosz, 1994, p. 81). Grosz's theorizing from within a very different socio-cultural context, i.e. the 1980s and 1990s, following the impact of the second-wave of twentieth century feminism, highlights the specific cultural limitations on Freud's account of the libido. Fromm's and Grosz's analysis can be further extended with regard to Freud's emphasis on the restrictive role of the ego: it has to "hold in check" the demands of the id (Freud, 1923b, p. 25), it has to "desexualise" or "sublimate" the libido of the id, it is itself at risk of punishment by the super-ego (Freud, 1923b, p. 55). Its "operations" are based on restriction, the maintenance of scarcity rather than production and expansion. Freud describes the workings of the ego as if they are objectively observable yet, as Fromm's and Grosz's claims highlight, his interpretations arise from a specific economic context.

The ethnocentric ego

Freud's theory of the ego was shaped not only by the economic context of middle-class Vienna, but also the context of white, European, Judeo-Christian culture. Despite his position as a Jewish man at a time of increasing discrimination against Jewish people, Freud does not consider racial differences or the effects of racism in his conceptualisation of the ego in *The Ego and the Id* (1923). Although debates in relation to Freud's conceptions of femininity were waged in the 1920s and 1930s and are often returned to by feminist scholars (Walton, 1997, p. 223), there have been comparatively few challenges, particularly in the psychoanalytic field, to the unacknowledged racial assumptions which underpin Freud's theory of the ego. In the 1920s, Malinowski, an anthropologist, and in the 1950s, Fanon, a psychoanalyst, were among the first to challenge the institution of psychoanalysis on the grounds of its ethnocentrism. However, since the 1990s an increasing number of critiques have emerged questioning the implicit association within psychoanalytic theory between psychological maturity and "white" European subjectivity (for example, Butler, 1993, Spillers,

1997, Walton, 1997). The paucity of critiques is undoubtedly linked to an understandable assumption by many people from black and other ethnic minorities that psychoanalysis has nothing to offer them. Since psychoanalysis is founded on a particular universalising conception of white European subjectivity, and since very few black people are accepted on to psychoanalytic psychotherapy trainings, doubts about its relevance to the experiences of people and some minority ethnic backgrounds are well founded.

The focus on sexual difference in psychoanalytic theorising arises from the presupposition that sexual difference is *the* fundamental difference between human beings, more fundamental than racial difference. Butler (1993) and Walton (1997) contest this, arguing that sexual and racial difference are instead articulated *through* one another and that neither difference is primary. According to Walton, it is assumed that the male-female binary is universal since not everyone is presumed to have been affected by a black-white binary in their development. However, as she points out, the acceptance of such a binary view does not depend on being raised in a mixed community of black and white people, although such an upbringing is more common than generally acknowledged; racial ideologies pervade the lives of both white Americans and Europeans "whose fantasmatic life is permeated by the Orientalist and Africanist ideologies that underwrite and justify what ... had become a long and vexed history of European colonialist expansion and decline" (Walton, 1997, p. 226). Yet, how such ideologies shaped white people's subjectivity was not recognised by psychoanalysts since "race" was conceived of as "blackness", as primitive and, as having nothing to do with "civilised" white subjectivity.

Malinowskis's early challenge to Freud is directed specifically at Freud's assumption that the Oedipus complex is universal. He argues that his account of it

> corresponds essentially to our patrilineal Aryan family with the developed *patria potestas*, buttressed by Roman law and Christian morals, and accentuated by the modern economic conditions of the well-to-do bourgeoisie (in Jones, 1928, p. 365).

For Malinowski, Freud's theorising of the Oedipus complex only applies to a specific middle-class, patriarchal, Christian context with a legal system inherited from the Romans. Ironically, Malinowski's critique, while recognising that there are culturally specific forms of family organisation underpinned by particular religious or other cultural values, does not consider the implications of his own interpretation with regard to Freud's position as a Viennese Jew. Fanon also argues against the universality of the Oedipus complex, claiming that in the French Antilles, for example, no neurosis associated with the complex can be identified in ninety-seven per cent of the families (Fanon, 1952, p. 152).

Freud's theorising of the Oedipus complex is central to his account of ego development. As Malinowski and Fanon point out, it presupposes a specific configuration of familial relations and patterns of childcare specific to white Western culture at the time of Freud's writing and assumed to be universal. Freud's failure to consider race, ethnicity, or racism with regard to the formation of the ego in his account of the ego in *The Ego and the Id* reflects his enrootedness in Enlightenment thought. As I have outlined, Enlightenment thought affirms an essential unity, founded on "reason", of all individuals beyond what are regarded as superficial cultural differences. It does not allow for the multiplicity and diversity of cultural languages, institutions and practices in which individuals are located and which shape their various intersubjective relations. These may be radically different from the white European model, which Freud presupposes.

Freud, furthermore, does not recognise the extent to which his account of ego development is predicated on an excluded black "Other", which is operative within white Western institutions, as much through an absence of black people in any given context as much as through their presence. Hammonds argues, for example, that a consequence of this is that black women's sexuality is relegated to "the irreducibly abnormal category in which there are no distinctions between homosexual and heterosexual women" (Hammonds, 1994, p. 138). Subjectivity is unavoidably shaped by the institutions, traditions, languages and practices of a particular culture. If these are shot through with discriminatory attitudes towards blackness, both implicit and explicit, all subjectivities will be consequently marked by these.

A consideration of how subjectivity is racialized once again raises the question of how subjectivity is shaped by the wider culture.

For Freud, the child's conscience (his super-ego or ego-ideal) is constituted primarily through his relation with his father and the dissolution of the Oedipus complex. It is later influenced by through the child's relations with other authority figures. In Butler's view, it is possible to extend Freud's concept of the ego-ideal with its role of regulating social norms to include that of maintaining particular cultural expectations with regard to race and gender (Butler, 1993, pp. 182–183). For example, she argues that the norm of whiteness in white culture is regulated through the ego-ideal. However, this claim fails to take into account the extent to which, from birth on, all the child's relations are informed by particular practices, which are unavoidably underpinned by specific cultural values with regard to race and skin colour.

Embodied subjectivity

Butler's rewriting of Freud's concept of the super-ego hinges on its being founded on a notion of power being imposed from "above". As I have discussed above, Freud's account of the role of the super-ego assumes that ideas, wishes and feelings which are acultural and pre-linguistic arise from the id and are then mediated by the ego under the scrutiny of the super-ego. How do such ideas, wishes and feelings come into being except as already located within a cultural context?

Merleau-Ponty who wrote *Phenomenology of Perception* in 1945, just over twenty years after Freud's *The Ego and the Id*, does not, in contrast to Freud, avoid issues of race with regard to subjectivity. He argues that our embodiment itself is culturally and historically specific since, as "intentional" subjects we are always already *in* the world. By "intentional" Merleau-Ponty means that consciousness is always consciousness *of* the world and we are thus, as subjects, always oriented towards the world (Merleau-Ponty, 1962, p. xviii). His concept of embodiment challenges the Cartesian dualisms which pervade Freud's account:

> The union of soul and body is not an amalgamation between two mutually external terms, subject and object, brought about by arbitrary decree. It is enacted at every instant in the movement of existence (Merleau-Ponty, 1962, pp. 88–89).

Just as his notion of "embodiment" undermines dualistic distinctions between body and mind, it also challenges those between internal and external, subject and world. Neither simply subjects or objects, our bodies are "our general medium for having a world". (Merleau-Ponty, 1962, p. 146). They are open to the world and through them the world is given form and meaning. The body is a condition of the world's existence because it is through our bodies that the world appears to us. As a phenomenologist, Merleau-Ponty is concerned primarily with "a direct description of our experience as it is," rather than a search for explanations in terms of causes (Merleau-Ponty, 1962, p. vii).

Although Merleau-Ponty is influenced by Freud (see, for example, Merleau-Ponty, 1962, pp. 157–158) he does not make use of Freud's notion of the ego. His theorising of embodiment challenges many of the assumptions on which Freud's conceptualisation hinges. In *The Ego and the Id* Freud makes, for him, the rare claim that "the ego is first and foremost a bodily ego" (Freud, 1923, p. 26). By this he means that the ego is derived from "bodily sensations" and it is therefore a mental "projection of a surface of the body" (Freud, 1923, p. 26). This remains undeveloped but, as it stands, this conceptualisation appears to reflect the dualistic thought which I have identified as problematic and which Merleau-Ponty's account of "embodiment" aims to disrupt.

Merleau-Ponty's notion of embodiment arises from his rejection of naturalism. He praises Freud for his attempt to integrate sexuality and existence in his theorising of the libido as "what causes man to have a history" (Merleau-Ponty, 1962, p. 158), enabling individuals to establish themselves in different contexts. However, he also launches an impassioned critique against the naturalism and explanations in terms of causality which he considers restrictive in psychoanalysis:

> We refused, as we always will, to grant to that phallus which is part of the objective body, the organ of micturition and copulation, such power of causality over so many forms of behaviour … It is not the useful, functional, prosaic body which explains man; on the contrary, it is the human body which rediscovers its symbolic or poetic weight (Merleau-Ponty, 1970, p. 69).

Merleau-Ponty's critique of naturalism leads him to argue against Freud's universalising of the developmental stages in children's sexual development. He claims that the orifices designated by Freud as universally erotogenic represent just a few of the many possible ones current in cultures as yet unknown to us (Merleau-Ponty, 1964b). The notion of an ego constituted through Oedipal identifications, held by Freud to be universal, is thus at great variance with Merleau-Ponty's notion of an intentional embodied subject.

The value of Merleau-Ponty's account of the subject as intentional and embodied is highlighted with regard to race and ethnicity. For Merleau-Ponty, race and cultural differences are neither naturally acquired, nor are they a result of tensions between the ego and the ego-ideal. Instead, they arise from a subject's "style" of being in the world (Merleau-Ponty, 1962, pp. 143–144). This "style" arises through a person's intersubjective relations and the accumulation of a background of shared meanings which become embodied. For Merleau-Ponty, listening is itself a form of embodiment such that words are "not signs to be deciphered" but "the transparent envelope of a meaning within which (the subject) might live." (Merleau-Ponty, 1962, p. 133). For Merleau-Ponty, to live in an intersubjective context is to live within a linguistic context of words as well as gestures. The gestures we acquire and the way we live a situation are specific to the style of our particular culture. For Merleau-Ponty, this would include class:

> It is not enough for two conscious subjects to have the same organs and nervous system for the same emotions to produce in both the same signs. What is important is how they use their bodies, the simultaneous patterning of body and world in emotion (1962, p. 189).

Merleau-Ponty's account of subjectivity as intentional and embodied allows for cultural specificity and diversity to a much greater extent than Freud's account of the "ego". It challenges dualistic distinctions between "internal" and "external" worlds and situates the subject within a world of language, gestural and spoken, allowing for the embodiment of different cultural meanings. Merleau-Ponty undermines naturalistic conceptions of subjectivity. He does not theorise an "inner" world of instinctual impulses which are harnessed by the id under the watchful eye of the "super-ego". Instead, he argues that sexuality is interfused with existence and does not exist as a specific excitation that lies outside and prior to the rest of our existence. It is historically and culturally specific and cannot be adequately theorised within the limitations of universal developmental stages in which the Oedipus complex is held to be pivotal.

How analysts conceptualise subjectivity has enormous conse-quences for their practice. Any notion of subjectivity is, as we have seen in this discussion of Freud's and Merleau-Ponty's accounts, underpinned by values arising from within a particular cultural context. If analysts rely uncritically on Freud's notion of the ego and the centrality of the Oedipus complex, this has consequences for their work with homosexual patients: they will be interpreted as being arrested in their sexual development and the possibilities for living happily in same-sex relationships will be foreclosed by the analyst. Furthermore, the analyst will not be open to the specific meanings same-sex relationships have for those patients and how identities as "lesbian or gay" are themselves socially and culturally specific. As I argue in Chapter Two, psychoanalytic theorising does not distinguish between the same-sex sexualities of, for example, upper-class married white women such as Virginia Woolf and Vita Sackville-West and that of a black working class woman who identi-fies as a lesbian queer contemporaneously.

A consideration of my work with a patient, Elaine, highlights the limitations of adhering to Freud's Enlightenment conceptuali-sation of the ego and the importance of being open to differences and the possibility of multiple identifications in relation to gender, race, class, sexuality. Elaine was a twenty-seven year old mixed race lesbian, the only child of a Black Afro-Caribbean father and a white English mother. Her father was a building labourer who had been unemployed for long periods in Elaine's childhood. Elaine wanted analysis because she wanted to "put an end to" her bouts of anxi-ety and depression. She had a demanding job in a lesbian and gay youth project and felt constantly under pressure: however hard she worked and however successful she was she never felt she was achieving enough. Elaine had been with her present partner, Donna for two years.

Elaine had been unsure whether she would be able to trust me as a white analyst whom she assumed was middle class and heterosexual. She was afraid that I might see her lesbianism as a pathology and she also wondered if I could ever sufficiently understand how isolating and undermining her experiences of racism had been for her. She had been raised on a mainly white housing estate and was the only black child in her primary school class. However, it was in her secondary school, where there were other black pupils, that she felt most taunted and exposed in the face of gangs of white girls who would threaten her and call her "darkie" and "black face". Yet she also did not feel she really belonged with the black children, since her mother was white.

Elaine had felt unsupported by her parents in the face of this hostility and, it emerged, particularly abandoned by her father who had very high expectations of her. She felt that he was only ever interested in whether she was getting high enough marks at school. Elaine thought now that he had been desperately anxious for her to succeed where he had not, as a black immigrant in 1950s Britain. This also led him to deny and ignore her attempts to tell him about the racism to which she was subjected. Elaine described her relationship with him as being one where they were constantly "at war" and, in her adolescence, they were constantly engaged in bitter and intense political arguments. In her analysis an important dream revealed Elaine's unconscious longing to be closer to her father and to be accepted by him. She mentioned at this point how very painful it was to her that he would not accept her being lesbian.

As a teenager Elaine had had two short relationships with boys and, when she was twenty, had her first relationship with a woman. It was at this point that Elaine "came out" as a lesbian and became very involved in black lesbian politics. Two years later, she had a short sexual relationship with a black gay man. She kept this secret from her lesbian feminist friends for fear they would think that she was not a "proper" lesbian. It took Elaine a long time to talk about this to me for fear that I would neatly categorise her as bisexual. She decided with the consent of her lover that she would have a one-off sexual encounter with a man in an attempt to "sort it all out". The encounter highlighted for her both how much she loved Donna and wanted to stay with her and also how it was possible for her to experience sexual pleasure with men. She continued to feel she was living an impossible paradox since a "proper" lesbian was someone who had never been attracted to men. In response to my question as to why it was so important to know whether she was either lesbian or heterosexual more memories emerged about her experiences of racism and feeling that she belonged neither to the white nor the black groups of children.

As Elaine felt increasingly confident that I was taking seriously her feelings of denigration and exclusion by both black and white people it became possible to interpret her anxieties in the transference. She said that she often chastised herself for "not doing analysis properly" and thought that I must really think that she was "stupid". She wished she knew what expectations I had of her. I responded to her by saying "so you would be able either to meet these, or do battle with me, as you did with your father. Not knowing what I expect means you have no definition and without that you feel vulnerable and stupid".

As the work continued links emerged between Elaine's need for certainty and her wish to be a "proper" lesbian. For Elaine, uncertainty and incompleteness in many aspects of her life were associated unconsciously with failure. She spoke at this time of her difficulties in being spontaneous and how she admired and envied people like her lover who were. For Elaine, spontaneity was associated with the risk of being "stupid", "silly" or "wrong".

Two years into her analysis Elaine began to risk more spontaneity in her relation with me, beginning with her admission that she often thought that I saw her as "stupid", she joined a Latin-American dance class with her lover. At first she was extremely nervous, feeling awkward and out of time. Then, suddenly in one class she felt an enormous shift and she found she was carried by the music in time with her partner. She was also amazed at the individuality of all the women dancing, despite dancing the same dance. I acknowledged how important it was for her to discover her own spontaneity and individuality in relation to the other dancers, and how this became possible only when she stopped thinking about "getting it right".

In working with Elaine I did not interpret her lesbianism as being "caused" by her feelings of disappointment in relation to her father, forcing her to identify with her father as a "masculine" lesbian.

(Cp. Freud's (1920) *Psychogenesis of a Case of Female Homosexuality,*
pp. 145–172). My work was not informed by Freud's notion of "ego
maturity", achieved through the working through of this relationship and the restoration of her heterosexuality. Nor did I collude
with her search for her "true" identity, whether lesbian, bisexual or
heterosexual, black or white. It was important for Elaine to see that
her anxiety about being a "proper" lesbian was connected to her
desperate need for certainty and perfection. This arose partly from
her father's high expectations of her, stemming from his experiences
as a black immigrant. It also arose from a cultural context which is
saturated with fixed notions of sexual identity as well as of white
subjectivity being superior.

If I had adhered to Freud's notion of the ego as acultural and
ahistorical I would not have been sensitive to the way in which
her experience of her subjectivity shifted between and across a
number of different positions as "black", "mixed race", "lesbian"
and "working class" and "heterosexual" and was shaped both in
response to and as a resistance to different forms of discrimination.
It was through my reading of Foucault that I was able to be attentive
to her different experiences of her subjectivity (or subjectivities).
I recognised that her own difficulty in accepting that the fluidity
of her subjectivity reflected the constraints in Freud's theorising of
the ego as universal and heterosexual. Since she had been raised
in a white European culture her view of subjectivity was inevitably shaped by the dominant discourse of Enlightenment thought to
which Freud, in his account of the ego, adhered. Merleau-Ponty's
account of embodied subjectivity was crucial in enabling me to
acknowledge the enormous importance to Elaine of being carried
with her partner by the music. It crystallized the possibility of
movement, of moving beyond the dualisms of "inner" and "outer",
and the finding of a unique gestural language which could also be
shared with others.

How analysts conceptualise "ego maturity" will affect their
sensitivity to the specific intersubjective worlds of their black
patients *and* their white patients and the effects of class position,
gender and institutionalised racism on these. For many analysts
such awareness in the consulting room is dismissed as "a collapse
into sociology", a failure to perceive the ego-identifications arising from early relations with parental figures, as if these figures

were not themselves located within a wider cultural context. Merleau-Ponty's account with his challenge to the distinctions between "internal" and "external" worlds in the constitution of our subjectivity, by contrast, acknowledges that subjectivity is always contextual and that differences are lived and embodied through and in the world in a multiplicity of ways. If analysts really attend to the details of how patients live the textures of their unique worlds with an openness to diversity, multiplicity, complexity and contradictions it will be evident that these cannot be contained within Freud's notion of the ego and its parental identifications.

CHAPTER SIX

Subjects of perversion

Noreen O'Connor

Every interpretation in analytical work is informed by a particular conception of the "subject". These conceptions often remain unexamined and unconscious on the part of analysts. I shall focus on the concept of perversion since it raises crucial questions regarding subjectivity and it has thus been the site of much debate among modernists and post-modernists. As I discussed in Chapter One, both modernists and post-modernists agree that individuals exist in different cultures and traditions and that they have specific histories. However, modernists believe that, although history and culture influence us, there are, nevertheless, universal, objective, standards of truth and goodness. If we achieve these we will live a healthy and happy life. Post-modernists disagree that any such universally foundationally rational rules or standards can be known outside of the specificity of the individual's life, culture, and historicity. Both these strands are discernible within Freud's theorising.

My aim in this chapter is to highlight the importance for analysts of reflecting critically on how their view of the subject informs their work. I shall discuss Freud's theory of fetishism and also Joel Whitebook's modernist interpretation of Freud as points of comparison with my own. Through discussion of some analytic work with a man whom I shall call Nigel, I shall reflect on the drawbacks of both these approaches. I shall argue against the notion that the task of analysis is the development of a more rationally integrated self-knowledge. On the contrary, I believe that my aim as an analyst is to enable the patient to live with ambiguity, complexity and uncertainty. Furthermore, the contribution of post-modernists to a conception of the subject as contingent can enable us to respond more sensitively to the historical and cultural specificity of individuals' experiences.

The tale of the blue ribbon

Nigel, a young man in his mid-twenties, presented for analysis because, in his words, he felt "very low" and had been so for some time. He was an intelligent and successful businessman, and he said that he worked with other young people like himself in the City (London's financial centre). Nigel had confided in a male friend about feeling so dragged down; he thought it stemmed from the ending of his relationship with his girlfriend. His friend suggested that he should seek therapy and Nigel had felt a sense of relief at the prospect of finding someone to help him. From a middle-class Welsh Methodist family, he was the youngest child with two older brothers and a sister who was the eldest. Nigel was in twice a week analysis for two and a half years.

In the early months of our work together Nigel expressed his intense anxiety at his recurrent and terrifying thoughts that he would die. He spoke about his family and, in particular, his mother whom he adored. She had very high moral standards, which Nigel said, he felt he always fell short of. His father did not rate much; he did not feel that he had a relationship with him. He admitted hesitantly that, since his anxieties had begun, he often longed to be a little boy again and he remembered feeling safe as he curled against his mother. Nigel compared himself to his brothers: they were "normal blokes" interested in football, cars, and women who would stay out all night. Moreover, unlike himself, they were not at all in thrall to their mother's high moral standards. They would shout and argue vehemently with her.

After several months of analysis, the adored mother of Nigel's childhood emerged as cold, domineering and restrictive. He felt very guilty about acknowledging this but he felt she must have been justified because he felt he was "bad". In the transference he experienced me as highly censorious in relation to his sexuality. He saw me as an older woman, like his mother, who was potent yet castrated, able and not able to help him and out to destroy his own potency. Nigel, nevertheless, was able to speak of his pain at losing his girlfriend. He was ashamed and embarrassed that, although he loved her, he could not make love to her since he was impotent with her. His fears that this was because he was gay emerged through his increasingly negative transference to me: he accused me of being homophobic. He began to give lengthy accounts of the virtues of his gay friends whom, he had decided, I would despise as "perverts". For him, he insisted, they were the most "together" people he knew. Nigel was now socializing almost exclusively with these friends and reflected about "coming out" himself. This possibility was full of fraught excitement: at last he would have a lover of his own and, most importantly, his mother would disown him. He could be rid of her and her sermons. The notion that he was gay seemed to relieve the strength of his anxieties about his sexual identity.

Eighteen months into his analysis Nigel arrived at a session, deeply distraught, saying that he wanted to kill himself. He had come to the session because he wanted to let me see the pain he was in. He described how he had "come out" to his friends, who had all been pleased for him. They had all gone to a gay club where one of his "so-called mates" tried to have sex with him. Since this had repulsed and terrified him there was no future for him: he wasn't straight and he wasn't gay. Furthermore, he felt that he didn't know who or what he was. He wondered if I as his analyst knew what he thought. He said that his mother used to know what he thought and she would tell him that he was her "baby". Nigel repeatedly spoke of his terror of losing his mind. I wondered aloud whether "losing his mind" felt like the disintegration of his existence, of his bodily existence. Nigel responded by speaking of his longing to be "out of it", free of the conflict of not knowing what he was. In an abstracted moment I wondered: "Why do you think that you should know what you are?" Long silence. "But then what do I know?" Nigel enquired. "You know the taste of tea and coffee, the colour of the sky on a summer's morning, the smile on the face of a friend". Silence. "You mean it's just living, just living every day?" he said.

Shortly after this session Nigel risked exposing the pain of his real pleasure. He arrived at a session and he sobbed and shook. In a low voice he confessed that he was afraid that he was really a transvestite. As a little boy he got excited at fondling his mother's knickers. He progressed to wearing them when she was out. Nigel's big secret was that he still dressed up in women's underwear and he had never told anybody this. This disclosure gave Nigel great relief and he expressed warm feelings for me as his analyst. He then went on to explain with great embarrassment that what gave him the excitement necessary to ejaculate was the tying of a piece of blue satin ribbon around his penis. Although he was embarrassed when talking of this he was also triumphant. It emerged that this triumph was derived from his having a secret pleasure, one which only he knew about. However, I wondered to myself whether he would be able to live with the revelation of this pleasure or whether it would destroy him.

One day, after months of speaking of his pleasure, Nigel announced with dismay that his piece of satin had lost its tarnish and no longer "did the trick". He went into a period of overwhelming depression and apathy, such that, he said, it wasn't even worth killing himself. We agreed to increase his sessions to four-times a week. Nigel began to realise that that his despair at his embodied existence co-existed with an unconscious and productive anger and revenge at his mother. He was furious that she wanted him to remain a baby so he couldn't be masculine like his brothers. Wearing the satin ribbon expressed his revenge towards her for confining his sexuality to "a wank with a ribbon". At the same time, the anger and revenge expressed in his secret pleasure also connected him to his mother. On occasions, in speaking of his secret, Nigel became very angry with me, demanding to know what sort of man I thought he was.

For Nigel, his secret pleasure was not only a response to his mother's demands on him and his father's absence. During this stage of his analysis he began to reflect on the cultural interpretations of gender and sexuality in the tightly knit Methodist community in which he had been raised. He reflected on how rigid these had been and much they had constrained him: he said that he knew too well what they considered to be the differences between men and women and such knowledge "left him nowhere".

Several months later Nigel spoke of his loneliness. Even though he had good company there was something missing. He felt he had "a fairly mundane life", but he didn't regret the loss of his secret drama. He then began to speak about a young woman colleague, who "fancied" him. He liked her a lot but felt nervous about going out with her. Over time they became closer and this was a revelation to him. Nigel found that he loved their physical intimacy and the ease and pleasure of this was, he said, a revelation. The world was alive and he no longer had to hide.

Freud's perversion

From a Freudian perspective this young man's presenting clinical material would be diagnosed as perverse. His fetish would be interpreted as arising from a conflict in relation to his masculinity. In his "Three Essays on the Theory of Sexuality" (1905d) Freud argued that there was no difference in the sources of neurotic symptoms and perversions. They are all generated by sexual wishes which are subject to repression. What distinguishes a "perversion" is that, unlike a neurotic symptom, which is disguised through symbolism, it is directly acted out. He thus defines perversions as "sexual activities which either (a) *extend*, in an anatomical sense, beyond the regions of the body that are designed for sexual union, or (b) *linger* over the intermediate relations to the sexual object which should normally be traversed rapidly on the path towards the sexual aim" (Freud, 1905d, p. 150).

Perversion, for Freud, arises specifically from the little boy's inability and refusal to accept the difference between his and his mother's gender. Freud further develops his theory in his paper "Fetishism" (1927e) where he maintains that the fetish is paradigmatic in perversion. The fetish allows the boy to retain what, at a logical level, is contradictory, namely, that his mother does, yet does not, have a penis. Freud explains that the holding of these two positions arises from "disavowal" whereby the ego splits to allow two contradictory attitudes to persist simultaneously without affecting each other. Freud argues that, whereas repression defends the ego against the imperious demands of the id, disavowal defends it against the demands of external reality. Thus, in repression, the split is between the ego and the id and, in disavowal, the split is within the ego. According to Freud, the fetish arises as a response to the traumatic anxiety experienced by the boy when he discovers that his mother does not have a penis and assumes that she is castrated. This recognition generates anxiety that he too will be castrated, and leads him to conclude that his mother both has, and does not have, a penis. The fetish plays the role of the missing penis and allows the fetishist to maintain that women are not castrated, that castration does not exist and that he is, therefore, not at risk. It is this reassurance that enables him to experience orgasmic pleasure. The fetish thus "remains a token of triumph over the threat of castration and a protection against it" (Freud, 1927e, p. 152). Furthermore, according to Freud, the fetish also serves to ward off the homosexuality, which arises in response to the fear of castration. The boy's insistent belief that his mother has a penis prevents him from resolving his Oedipus complex and taking up a truly heterosexual position.

Freud maintains that "*in every instance*, the meaning and the purpose of the fetish turned out, in analysis, to be the same" (my emphases) (Freud, 1927e, p. 154). Yet, as my description of my work with Nigel highlights, such a claim forecloses on the specific meanings of certain forms of sexual behaviour for each individual, including their socio-cultural specificity. For Nigel, there is no evidence that, in his use of the blue ribbon, he wished to retain a notion of his mother as "having a phallus", alongside his knowledge that she did not. The blue ribbon served another purpose: it allowed him to express his rage at her desire for him to remain infantile, her "little boy". In re-enacting what he felt had been done to him, he was in control and he was able to symbolically punish his mother for causing him to be like this. This re-enactment also connected him to her. Furthermore the blue ribbon also expressed the contradictory demands that his mother and his religious community had made on him as a boy. They all knew who or what he should be and what he should think. If only he could know who or what he really was, he would be free of all their definitions and demands. Nigel was triumphant at having this secret pleasure because it was one of the few things in his life that he knew to be his very own. This "something" that was his very own cannot be captured by the notion of the phallus: it was the site of Nigel's articulation of his rage and a creative response to the contradictory demands on his masculinity.

If I had adhered to Freud's interpretation of the fetish I would have bypassed many of the questions that were preoccupying Nigel. I would also have been treating Nigel in the very same way that he had been treated by his mother and the church: they both knew what he thought and told him what he should think. The crucial shift in Nigel's analysis occurred in response to my interpretation, which took the form of a question, as to why he thought that he should know what he was. It opened a space between us for ambiguity and uncertainty, and possibilities of other forms of "knowing" which allowed Nigel to speak of what been, hitherto, unspeakable. This interpretation was informed by a notion of subjectivity as fluid and shifting and not as something which can be known. It was thus a challenge to normative notions of subjectivity in which the "normal" subject knows himself to be heterosexual or, at the very least, "knows" his sexual orientation as either "straight" or gay. Furthermore, my interpretation was informed by a commitment to hold open questions of what constitutes masculinity and femininity.

In my responses to Nigel my aim was not that he should relinquish his fetish. I do not hold the view that to give up a fetish is necessarily a sign of having achieved maturity: I do not see the task of analysis as providing a "cure" of this type. Furthermore, this would also be a denial of the cultural specificity of the notion of the fetish and the value judgements that designate the fetish as "unnatural" sexual behaviour. What was most important was that I offer Nigel the possibility of articulating his struggles and his despair in their unconscious aspects. The "success" of the analysis lay in his feeling less haunted by the persecutory voices of his past and discovering that it is possible to live with ambiguity and uncertainty. That Nigel went on to have a heterosexual relationship without his blue satin ribbon is not, in my view, a measure of the success of the therapy.

Perversion and utopia?

The view of subjectivity which informs my work is influenced by post-modernist theorising. This is characterized by a critique of the Enlightenment's autonomous and self-legislating self in favour of a notion of the subject as shaped by the specific socio-historical context. Post-modernists thus reject universalising theories, maintaining that, on the contrary, knowledge and truth are perspectival. Some post-modernists argue that there are strands of post-modernism in Freud's theorising, citing, for example, his problematisation of heterosexuality. For Freud it is not "given", it has to be achieved through a process of various precarious identifications. (See Freud, 1905d, *Three Essays On the Theory of Sexuality*).

By contrast with post-modernist interpretations of Freud, Joel Whitebook, writing as a philosopher and a psychoanalyst, claims that what is central to Freud's agenda is the exploration of the "irrational" in order to integrate it into an expanded notion of rationality. Whitebook is in agreement with what he reads as Freud's aim of psychoanalysis, namely the ego's integration of the instinctual forces from which it has been hitherto defended: "Rather than abandoning the standpoint of the ego altogether, the deconstruction of naive consciousness can instead initiate a process of creating, through the work of psychoanalysis and in alliance with the analysand's observing ego, a more adequate ... ego/consciousness" (Whitebook, 1995, p. 131). Whitebook thus insists that Freud was a modernist, a theorist of an autonomous, universally rational subject.

Whitebook characterizes post-modernism as a symptom of the groundlessness of modern living which, he argues, is expressed by identification with the irrational and the transgressive—an idealisation of romanticism. By contrast, he favours "a concept of the non-coercive integration of the self ... a necessity for countering post-modernism's manic and one-sided celebration of generalized dissolution and dispersion ..." (Whitebook, 1995, p. 262). Whitebook implies that post-modernist readings of Freud deny the reality of trauma and its effects. He argues that these "utopian" psychoanalytical positions on subjectivity operate with the same denial and disavowal that Freud attributes to perversion. They are thus identified with the idealisation of perverse sexuality and what is excluded are problems of trauma, disavowal, and aggression.

This raises the question as to whether my interpretations of Nigel's "secret pleasure" denied his pain. In my view, interpretations informed by a post-modernist critique of the rational subject are not incompatible with a response to a person's suffering. Throughout the my work with Nigel I remained attentive to his conflicts and his despair. Although I bore in mind the notion that the fetish is itself a culturally and historically specific term, I did not assume that what was required was for Nigel to perceive his secret pleasure as liberatory and thus idealise transgression. What post-modernist thought enabled me to do was to challenge the universalising features of Freud's theory of the fetish and to attend more sensitively to Nigel's suffering in its historical and cultural specificity.

Whitebook's critique raises a further question with regard to the efficacy of the analytic work with Nigel. Nigel was terrified of what he did not know and wondered how to know it. He did not know who or what he was and whether he was gay or straight. It might appear that Nigel's dilemma would have been resolved more satisfactorily if I had taken Whitebook's view of the aim of psychoanalysis. The aim of the analysis for Nigel would have been the achievement of a rationally integrated self through the strengthening of his ego. It seems to me that this would be to lead Nigel further in the direction of the belief system which confined him. Nigel's problem lay in his desire for knowledge and certainty as to who and what he was. As I have described in the case presentation it was crucial that I held open a space for ambiguity and uncertainty.

In his argument for the norm of subjectivity as integrated rationality Whitebook does not address the radical aspects of Freud's theorising, such as his problematisation of gender differences, heterosexuality, homosexuality, and lesbianism. The integrated self that Whitebook advocates seems to be genderless and non-sexual. He also does not address the fact that some psychoanalytic writers on perversion insist that homosexuality and lesbianism are, by definition, pathological and in need of cure.

Conclusion

Nigel's analysis ended when he discovered that he could live and that living was not a matter of hiding, denying, inventing, and thinking his life. I believe that this was possible for Nigel because I did not adhere to a notion of maturity in the subject as the integration of rationality, the achievement of heterosexuality, or the certainty that one is a man or a woman. I did not hold back from the challenge of questions such as how can human embodiment be known? Why ask that question? What is the relationship between embodiment and discourse? Is there an essential femininity and masculinity?

I have argued that post-modernist analyses of identities and differences can enable analysts to open out such questions and heighten their sensitivity to the specificity of their patients. The interpretation of differences need not be exclusively confined to a rigid theorising of psychic development. Furthermore, the interpretation of differences does not preclude careful recognition of and attention to the traumas which confine people to a rigid and compulsive life of satisfactions, generating self-hatred and isolation from others. It matters very much in practice how an analyst conceives of subjectivity, masculinity, femininity, sexuality, homosexuality. As Joanna Ryan and I argue in *Wild Desires and Mistaken Identities*, "the history of psychoanalysis does not encourage confidence in its ability to change and adapt, except by fissure and expulsion, but perhaps the pluralism that is now demanded and evident in so many other areas of thought and theory could extend to psychoanalysis" (O'Connor & Ryan, 1993, p. 271).

CHAPTER SEVEN

(Dis)continuous identities and the time of the other

Mary Lynne Ellis

How individuals "live" time in all its dimensions is pivotal to the analyses of subjectivity of philosophers writing from phenomenological, existential, and deconstructive perspectives. Through my reflections on the theories of temporality presented by Heidegger, Merleau-Ponty, Foucault, and Levinas, I expand on some of the themes and questions posed by such theories.

I particularly focus on their differing positions in relation to the question of whether the subject has a continuous identity through time and also the subject's relation to others' time. In critically presenting their very different positions one of my aims is also to highlight the diverse assumptions operative in such theories. My interest is in how these theories are constructed and how particular theories might illuminate a particular patient's variable and conscious and unconscious dilemmas in relation to time. I argue against the notion that there is one universal relation to time, whether as continuity or discontinuity, which must be achieved in order for the patient's suffering to be alleviated.

Calendar time, cosmological time and lived time

In considering the relevance of temporality to notions of subjectivity in analytical practices it is necessary to distinguish "lived time" from our ordinary conceptions of time as cosmological and as dateable. As Mann's (1924) novel, *The Magic Mountain*, so poignantly exemplifies, abstract notions of time as motion, as change, as linear or circular, or as dateable, can never encapsulate the temporality of human experience. Mann explores in fictional form the effects on patients in a sanatorium of the imposition of its particular time (the time of the doctors), a time which differs radically from that which is lived beyond its walls. In the sanatorium, the smallest unit of time is the month and, in decisions regarding the length of treatments for patients, doctors treat weeks as if they are only days.

Mann's reflections on time are voiced through the musings of the central character, Hans Castorp. Castorp's time as a patient under-lines for him that the time of the calendar, the units of minutes, hours, days, weeks, months and years are "purely arbitrary, sheer conventions" (Mann, 1924, p. 66): the second hand on a watch may complete the same circuit each time to indicate the passing of a minute, but our *experience* of the time it takes is variable. For Castorp, most often, days in the sanatorium are exceedingly long yet, retrospectively, in their emptiness, they seem to "scurry by like dead leaves" (Mann, 1924, p. 105) indistinguishable from today, blending into "the always" (Mann, 1924, p. 546). Since the sana-torium is up in the mountains even the calendar cycle of the sea-sons is non-existent: there are spring and autumn *days*, burning hot summer days in winter, and snowfall in the summer, all incongru-ent with the seasons designated arbitrarily by the calendar. Mann's novel conveys vividly the operations of institutionalization in tem-poral terms and its alienating effects on the patients' subjectivity: time is organized such that "one should get used to things, even if the getting used consisted in getting used to not getting used" (p. 349).

The questions which Mann raises through his character, Castorp, regarding the relation between cosmological time, dateable time and "lived time" extend far beyond the particular context of the institution that he describes in the novel. The impossibility of an exact correlation between, for example, the times of sunrise, sunset, and planetary movements, and any system of calendar time indicate that time and dates are relative, not absolute. In his Special Theory and his later General Theory of Relativity (1911) Einstein argues that time is affected by mass and also by relative speed.

Osborne argues that calendars themselves are "socially specific versions of cosmological time" (Osborne, 1995, p. 67). He traces the connection between the development of capitalism and the establishment of world standard-time: time synchronization in the organization of transport and communications became crucial to the success of capitalism. However, as Osborne points out, world standard-time is no more than one abstract measure alongside the myriad of other diverse time measurements existent in local social practices.

The question of how individuals "live" time, as highlighted in Mann's *The Magic Mountain* is a major theme in modern European philosophical thought. Time is neither objective, nor observable as something "outside" the subject. We are always "in time" or as Merleau-Ponty (1945) claims, we *are ourselves* time (see below). The variability of our lived experiences of time is, as this book argues, of particular relevance to practising analysts. I begin with a discussion of Heidegger's theorizing of our ordinary conception of time. His work has been of particular influence on the theorizing and practices of existential analysts such as Binswanger and Boss.

Heidegger's future-time

Heidegger (1962) emphasizes that clock-time, as public time, is necessary and that temporality is the condition for its discoverability and its necessity. He argues against common-sense views of time as a sequence of "nows" (originating with Aristotle) and claims that these obscure the dateability and significance of time. Heidegger challenges dichotomies between the self and the world and theorizes Dasein (the "Being" of persons) as always already in the world through its "thrownness" (Heidegger, 1962, p. 174). Dasein is grounded in temporality, constituted by the phenomena of the future, the past and the present. He designates these dimensions the "ecstases" (Heidegger, 1962, p. 416) of temporality. In designating them as "ecstases", Heidegger means that they "stand out". Dasein is carried beyond itself, transcending the world, through the unity of the ecstases. However, the beyond to which it is carried is not limitless; each of the ecstases has a different "horizontal schema" (Heidegger, 1962, p. 416). Dasein's relation to its future is disclosed in the horizontal schema of *"for-the-sake-of-itself"*, its relation to the past is defined by the horizontal schema of "thrownness", and the horizontal schema for the present is framed by the *"in-order-to"* (Heidegger, 1962, p. 416). Each of these dimensions temporalize themselves in relation to the other dimensions.

In contrast to much psychoanalytic theorizing which, with the exception of Jung's, Lacan's and Winnicott's (see Ellis, 2008), prioritizes the past as most formative of the subject, Heidegger prioritizes the future. In his analysis of "care" which he defines as "concern and solicitude" he distinguishes between "willing" and "wishing" which both signify a particular relation to the future. In "willing", one's "potentiality-for-Being" is unavoidably modified by the limitations posed by the social context, i.e. "everydayness" (Heidegger, 1962, p. 239 and pp. 421–422). "Wishing" is constituted by "being-ahead-of-oneself" such that whatever is available is "never enough" (Heidegger, 1962, p. 239) and he associates this with the notion of "hankering" and "addiction" (Heidegger, 1962, p. 240). In addiction, all other possibilities of being are subsumed in the craving for intoxication.

Heidegger argues that authentic temporality depends on our recognition of the finiteness of our individual "Being-towards-death". Our awareness of our own mortality structures our relation to the present and the past. In the face of death, Dasein "stands before itself in its ownmost potentiality-for-being" (Heidegger, 1962, p. 294). Concepts of time as a series of "now" points imply an infinite continuity in which there is no death. If Dasein immerses itself in this everyday view of time, in flight from an acknowledgement of its own death, it loses itself: it is closed off from its authenticity and its potentiality. Dasein "is a 'not-yet' which any Dasein, as the entity which it is, has to be" (Heidegger, 1962, p. 288). According to Heidegger, anxiety is rooted in Dasein's fear about its potential individuality (see Ellis, 2008 for more discussion of this). For further clarification of Heidegger's arguments I recommend Rée's (1998) publication, *Heidegger, History and Truth In Being and Time* to the reader.

Heidegger's interpretation of the relationship between "authentic" living and our awareness of our own mortality resonates with the thoughts of a patient who had recently been diagnosed with an illness from which she might eventually die. She described how she had always lived in the future and that "now, as I don't know if I will have a future, I have to live in each moment". For her the future had been, in her words, "like a false self, an ideal self" and she felt that her focus on this had stopped her paying enough attention to her health in the present (of her recent past). Although she had been focusing on the future, this was a future conceptualized as being without death (without imperfection). Now death had revealed itself as a possibility in the future she could consider living in the present (which included taking up her past).

The problem with Heidegger's analysis of death is its individualism (Levinas 1947b and Osborne 1995). He claims that death is "By its very essence ... is in every case mine" (Heidegger, 1962, p. 284). Furthermore, others' interpretations of death deny its "own most possibility which is non-relational and not to be outstripped" (Heidegger, 1962, p. 307). Heidegger implies that an authentic relation to our own death and to our own existence is only possible if we repudiate the meanings derived from our experiences of others' dying and also the dominant social and religious discourses on death. As Osborne (1995) points out, there is a tension between the individualism within Heidegger's analysis of death and his emphasis on our "Being-with" others, even when we are alone, as an essential characteristic of Dasein (Heidegger, 1962, p. 156). However, despite this tension, Heidegger's acknowledgement that the knowledge of our own death ahead profoundly affects how we live our lives is, in my view, extremely important in psychoanalytic work with patients at any stage of their lives.

Osborne incisively discusses the relation between Heidegger's support of National Socialism in Germany and his philosophical theories, an issue which has been widely debated amongst modern European philosophers. He argues that Heidegger's position was not based on anti-semitism but rooted in his opposition to technology and mass industrialization. Osborne's analysis of the relation between National Socialism's stance as a "reactionary avant-garde" and Heidegger's theorizing of Being points to a problem in Heidegger's theorizing of time. In Osborne's view, these converge in their shared commitment to a "*return* to a new beginning" through a revival of the importance of tradition (Osborne, 1995, p. 172). He argues that this gives rise to a paradox in Heidegger's thought since it implies an originary sense of Being which is located beyond or before time and is, itself, the source of historicity. It is, of course, vitally important to be attentive to the reactionary aspects of Heidegger's thought and its political implications. Not withstanding this, there are many aspects of his work which can contribute to a consideration of the subject's experiences of temporality which are of value to practicing analysts.

The times of world-designs

The existential psychoanalyst Binswanger, a close friend and colleague of Freud's, was strongly influenced by Heidegger in his theorizing of subjectivity. He emphasizes the temporal modes of individuals' "Existential A Prioris" or "world-designs". According to Binswanger, a "world-design" is a mode through which Dasein is structured. Dasein's existence may be structured through one mode or through several, one or some of which are more dominant than others. Binswanger designates the term "Geworfenheit" ("thrownness") for a state of being constricted overwhelmed by a particular world-design. In psychosis the individual is completely overpowered by a single world design. Binswanger emphasizes that a world-design is revealed in the specificity of individuals' language. Furthermore, it is neither conscious nor unconscious: it lies beyond these dualisms. A world-design neither precedes subjectivity or imposes on an already existing subjectivity; a world-design is, rather, a relation to the world.

Binswanger draws on Von Gebsattel's notion of "lived time", differentiating it from the *experience of* time, and extends this in his concept of the "self-temporalizing of the existence" (Binswanger, 1946, pp. 301–302). By this he means that Dasein transcends itself in the ecstases of the future (the *"toward which"* or "being-ahead-of oneself"), the past (the *"upon which" or* "having-been"*),* and the present (the *"with which"* or *"*being-with") (Binswanger, 1946, p. 302). Existence is determined by both its future and its past, its "thrownness", such that "All futurity of the existence is therefore 'has-been' and all having-been is of the future" (Binswanger, 1946, p. 303). With Heidegger, Binswanger claims that the future dimension, however, is primary for Dasein since existence concerns being-able-to-be, which he equates with understanding. The present is given meaning through decisive action.

Throughout his clinical illustrations Binswanger analyses the individual's relation to the different temporal dimensions. He emphasizes, however, that the analyst's attunement to her/his patients' temporalities does not rely on their conscious or explicit articulation of how they live time. Binswanger's case-example concerning the suffering of a young woman whose world-design is structured by the temporal mode of continuity, is of particular relevance since the question of the continuity of subjectivity continues to preoccupy many psychoanalytic theorists (see below). Binswanger describes how, as a five year old girl, the young woman had experienced a panic attack and fainted after an incident when her heel separated from her shoe and got caught in her skate. From then on she had become overwhelmed with anxiety at any loosening of her heel, any talk of heels, or if anyone touched her heel.

In Binswanger's view, the young woman's world had shrunk to the one category of significance, namely "*continuity*, of continuous connection and containment" (Binswanger, 1946, p. 203). Any disruption to her world in the form of the new and unexpected was experienced as a suddenness that "explodes continuity, hacks it and chops it to pieces ... exposes it to the naked horror" (Binswanger, 1946, p. 204). Her phobia of heels was a way of safeguarding herself from this horror, the anxiety of existence itself, and the movement of time towards the future. Behind her fears of loose heels were birth phantasies which revealed her fears of separation from her mother. The young woman fixed herself in past time, the "already having-been-in" (Binswanger, 1946, p. 205). However, paradoxically, the more she constricted her world to preserve it from her anxiety, the more anxiety she felt in the face of a possible threat to this.

Binswanger vividly describes the structure of the young woman's experience of her world and her specific and troubling relation to time and change. He argues against a Freudian reduction of her phobia to her "predisposition" and proposes a more "anthropological angle" (Binswanger, 1946, p. 203). He contends that the birth phantasies were not phylogenetic but arose out of this young woman's particular "world-design". He challenges the notion that an overly intense pre-Oedipal tie to the mother might be the source of the young woman's world-design of continuity and her fear of suddenness. In his view such a causal explanation is inadequate. Instead he interprets the strength of this tie as arising from her world-design: her attachment to her mother was her way of having a "hold on the world" (Binswanger, 1946, p. 203).

As Needleman (1967) emphasizes, a world-design of continuity is not in itself necessarily problematic to an individual. What is problematic is the extent to this temporal mode restricts an individual's freedom to risk exploring other possibilities of living. I focus on the question of the importance of a sense of continuity through time in the light of current debates within psychoanalysis below. Firstly I want to consider the value and limitations of the notion of a "world-design". Laing (1961), for example, indicates that this concept does not sufficiently take into account the actual influence of others on an individual, whether in the present or the past. Certainly, the effects of, for example, living in a patriarchal society, are not addressed in Binswanger's case studies of women. Binswanger was unavoidably affected by his own "thrownness" into a time at which such analyses of gender were undeveloped. However, his theorizing and his case illustrations do not exclude a recognition of the effects of others; throughout they allow for an attentiveness to the particular and unique lived experience of an individual in all its intersubjective manifestations as revealed through their language.

Binswanger takes into account the extensiveness of an individual's world which cannot be completely circumscribed by notions of the drives, the intra-psychic, early development or immediate family relationships. It is important to stress, however, that in practice, it is equally essential, to be attentive to the significance of the moments at which an individual departs from his/her world-design. Although his emphasis on the specificity of an individual's language does allow for this, this aspect is not sufficiently developed by Binswanger.

Merleau-Ponty's lived present

Merleau-Ponty emphasizes the present temporal dimension over the future in his theorizing. Against Heidegger he argues that we can only perceive time from the point of view of the present: "it is always in the present that we are centred, and our decision starts from there" (Merleau-Ponty, 1962, p. 427). Merleau-Ponty rarely mentions the subject's mortality. He regards temporality as integral to the motility of the lived body: a bodily movement in the present always dovetails with a previous instant of movement and anticipates a future movement. Each movement contains within it the succession of the previous positions and the outline of those to come. We actively assume time non-reflectively: the human body belongs to or "includes" time. Furthermore, he emphasizes, our relation to time is intersubjective; we are alive to and share in the temporalities of others with their histories and future aspirations.

For Merleau-Ponty, time arises "from my relation to things" (Merleau-Ponty, 1962, p. 412). With Heidegger, he argues strongly against Aristotle's linear conception of time as a series of instances of "now". He also critically reflects on the common metaphor of time as a river flowing from past to future. He draws our attention to how, if an observer is introduced into this picture, those time dimensions are reversed. For example, a perception of a volume of water flowing forward with the current quickly becomes a past perception to the standing observer. Merleau-Ponty's view is interesting in the light of recent research (Nuñez, 2006) on the Aymara people who live in the Andes, in Chile. For the Aymara, the past is in front of them and the future is behind them. Nuñez speculates that the reason for this might be that their language emphasizes the visual. The past that they have "seen" (experienced) is therefore in front of their eyes. The future is behind as it is, as yet, hidden from view. It appears that such metaphors are culturally and/or historically specific.

Phenomenology is a method of describing experience, not an empirical, deductive, or inductive theory of the "reality" of our existence. As a phenomenologist Merleau-Ponty argues that time is perspectival: for the subject "the past is a former future and a recent present, the present an impending past and a recent future, the future a present and even a past to come" (Merleau-Ponty, 1962, p. 422). Time is a dimension of our existence, a "network of intentionalities" (Merleau-Ponty, 1962, p. 417) and we are carried forward by lines of "intentionality" which trace out the style of our futures. These lines do not originate in us; we are situated within a perceptual field which is run through with "retentions" and "protentions". "Retention" refers to the transition of a present moment into the past, whilst remaining present, and "protention" refers to the overlap between the present and the impending future moment. Although past, present, and future are distinguishable, they are nevertheless embraced within a single flux which is present. Furthermore, Merleau-Ponty argues that we must conceive of the subject as temporality itself, both thrusting and being thrust towards the future: "We must understand time as the subject and the subject as time" (Merleau-Ponty, 1962, p. 422).

Merleau-Ponty specifically addresses how the meanings of certain "symptoms" can be illuminated through a consideration of them as a reflection of the subject's conflictual relation to time (in any of its dimensions). This is vividly illustrated in his interpretations of a woman's loss of speech and appetite (a case of Binswanger's). The woman is no longer able to eat or to speak when her mother prohibits her from seeing a young man with whom she is in love. The young woman had previously lost her speech twice in her childhood, following firstly an earthquake and then another frightening experience. Merleau-Ponty argues against a Freudian interpretation which would interpret her later loss of speech as a young woman in terms of a fixation at the oral stage of sexual development. He claims that, on the contrary, what has become fixated for her is not only her sexual existence but her spoken relations with others. Her mother's action threatens to cut her off from the possibility of a future, just as her earlier frightening experiences also carried the threat of death and the loss of co-existence. Her loss of speech is a means of escape from the conflict; it is a refusal of co-existence and of life itself. Moreover, by not eating she is refusing to assimilate events that are part of the flow of existence; she is refusing to "swallow" her mother's prohibition from seeing the man whom she loves.

Merleau-Ponty's account imaginatively captures the specificity of this woman's relation to time and to language. An interpretation which reductively locates the source of her loss of speech and her appetite in a fixation at an early infantile stage of development does not adequately address the present conflict, namely between her own and her mother's desires, its connection to those past experiences where she feared losing her life, its threat to her future, and the shifting of her past perceptions in the light of her current experiences.

Merleau-Ponty (like Binswanger) does, however, fail to address the "time" of gender. From a Foucauldian perspective, the woman's inability to speak might be interpreted both as a powerful point of resistance and an (almost satirical) embodying of the silencing of her sexuality. This "silence" is required of her by her mother within the context of a time and a culture whose dominant discourses convey women's sexuality as threatening. She refuses to swallow the prohibition of these, as transmitted within her relationship with her mother. Although, from Merleau-Ponty's presentation of the case, we do not know enough about the young woman's relation to food and to her body-image, we might speculate on this in the light of the power of social discourses regarding historical and cultural expectations of women's body size. It is important to stress, however, the socio-historical context of Merleau-Ponty's writing, namely that of the mid twentieth century, not withstanding the groundbreaking work of Simone de Beauvoir in *The Second Sex* (1949), before the emergence of European and American feminist psychoanalytic perspectives on women's development.

Merleau-Ponty's view of temporality as synonymous with subjectivity and his theorizing of the subject's shifting relations to all three dimensions, each with their own temporal horizons, offers a valuable contribution to psychoanalytic practices. The stories of patients' experiences told in the present in the consulting room shift from present to past to future. Contained within each of these dimensions are other presents, pasts and futures, extending back and forwards through time. Merleau-Ponty's theorizing alerts us to the limitations of the naturalism of Freud's developmental theories and the constraints of Klein's prioritizing of the time of the baby.

Identities continuous in time?

In my critical presentation of Heidegger's, Binswanger's and Merleau-Ponty's theorizing of temporality my intention is to raise questions for psychoanalytic theorizing and practices. What conception of time with its transitions between the past, present, and future does the analyst bring to the psychoanalytic relationship? What normative assumptions about a "healthy" relation to time might be at play in the clinical work? Does the analyst take the view that, for example, an acceptance of temporal gaps and discontinuities is more psychically mature or, the converse, that the experience of a continuous sense of self through time is an aim of psychoanalytic work, as Winnicott argues?

According to Merleau-Ponty, drawing from Heidegger, "I" am "one single 'living cohesion' one single temporality, which is engaged from birth in making itself progressively explicit, and in confirming itself in each successive present present" (Merleau-Ponty, 1962, p. 407). There is no "I" external to this, an agent, which synthesizes perceptions taken in from a number of different perspectives. Nor is there an "I" which is consciously experienced in each act of perception. Rather, he argues, the unity of the "I" is "invoked" (Merleau-Ponty, 1962, p. 406) in the present and through this the unity of all my thoughts is achieved. Merleau-Ponty stresses that this unity does not depend on the retention of memory, since we do not in any physiological sense possess a store of memories which we have to consciously recall in order to affirm the existence of our past. We feel and assume the presence of our past.

Although the subject is a single "living cohesion", Merleau-Ponty does not deny that the subject is contextual; he argues that "Inside and outside are inseparable. The world is wholly inside and I am wholly outside myself" (Merleau-Ponty, 1962, p. 407). This means that we extend towards, are open to, and affected by the temporalities of others with their histories and future aspirations and we acquire backgrounds of shared meanings. There is therefore some fluidity implicit in Merleau-Ponty's concept of subjectivity: it is contextual and relational. However, it does not go far enough in allowing for the very radical breaks in self-continuity that are experienced by many individuals.

Hoffman (1989)'s autobiography, *Lost In Translation*, spans the years of Hoffman's childhood, firstly in post-war Poland and then, from the age of thirteen, in Canada, through to her adult life in New York. Her account is movingly punctuated by her reflections on the significance to her of her frequent experiences of gaps and discontinuities. Her departure from Poland in a ship bound for Canada marked for her the end of the "narrative of her childhood" (Hoffman, 1989, p. 95). Much later, as a student at Harvard she unexpectedly encounters a childhood friend from Poland. Looking together at an old photograph of themselves as children, they realize the impossibility of crossing "such a large time canyon" (Hoffman, 1989, p. 222). In her relationship with her mother, Hoffman is thrown back and fore across so many generational divides, she is conscious of how emigration has "bollixed up the time distances between us"

(Hoffman, 1989, p. 250). For her, memory "emits an intermittent glow" (Hoffman, 1989, p. 242) and, in revisiting Crakow, the town of her childhood, her past is revealed to her, reassuringly, as "only a story" (Hoffman, 1989, p. 242). Perceptions of the past are thus narratives which emerge in different ways at different times (see Ellis, 2008).

Hoffman warns of the dangers of nostalgia ("an ineffectual relationship to the past" in which time is static) and of alienation ("an ineffectual relationship to the present") as defences against discontinuities. (Hoffman, 1989, p. 242). In her personal psychoanalysis she realizes that these gaps, although at times a source of suffering, are also a source of her aliveness. Healing her suffering does not mean the development of a sense of herself as continuous. It also does not mean denying discontinuity. She discovers how to shift between Polish and English without sealing over their differences, and also without being split by them. The gaps are what sharpen her sensitivity to diversity. Many of Hoffman's references to experiences of time resonate with Merleau-Ponty's account but her attention to the inevitability and the value of the discontinuous is more congruent with Foucault's theorizing.

Foucault, who had been a student of Merleau-Ponty's, argues that any notion of continuous history erases occurrences such as sudden accidents and discoveries, which unavoidably cut across the continuous. His concern is with the relation between discourses and practices in relation to subjectivity. His methods are "archaeological" and "genealogical". The "archaeological" method is concerned not with whether discourses express the truth or make sense but with the rules that govern them. From this Foucault developed the "genealogical" method in order to thematize the relation between truth, values and practices. Genealogy is an approach to history which seeks out discontinuities as against continuity and rejects notions of fixed essences, underlying laws or metaphysical finalities. Counter to those historical narratives in which events have often been "rearranged, reduced, effaced in order to reveal (their) continuity", (Foucault, 1969, p. 8). Foucault argues for an attentiveness to the small shifts, gaps and crises in history.

According to Foucault, the notion of history as continuous is problematic. It relies on an assumption that the subject can be certain of restoring everything that has been lost, that everything will eventually be reconstituted in the unity of time, and that s/he will be able to absorb everything s/he perceives to be different. Foucault's critique is an implicit challenge to Merleau-Ponty's theorizing. As we have seen, Merleau-Ponty claims that, for the subject, the totality of his/her experience including the past and anticipation of the future is operative within every present thought and action. For Foucault, this would be to place the subject as the source or origins of historical development. Against Merleau-Ponty's view that a person whom we know in the present is the same person as we met in the past, Foucault (1969) poses the example of Nieztsche. He argues that there cannot be the same relation between the name Nieztsche and his philosophical writings, his letters, notebooks, sketches and laundry lists.

An interesting conceptualization of the relation between continuity and discontinuity of identities through time emerged in a professional development workshop I ran for art therapists entitled "Image and Embodiment", focusing particularly on the work of Merleau-Ponty. In response to my reflections on Foucault's challenge to Merleau-Ponty, one of the participants used the time allocated for personal artwork to explore this question. She cut a spiral into a square piece of black paper. Flat, with the spiral cut into it, the paper had one identity. When she pulled at the centre of the paper, the spiral extended outwards in a three-dimensional spiral, revealing a radically different identity. Both these, and also the shapes in between, depending on how far the participant pulled the spiral were equally possible from the same piece of paper. The participant's work offered a creative solution for a conceptualization of identity as simultaneously continuous and discontinuous.

The different positions taken up by Merleau-Ponty, Hoffman, and Foucault alert us to the importance for analysts of both acknowledging and questioning the assumptions that they make about the relation between time and subjectivity and the implicit value judgements they attach to these. How do these influence their aims for the patient? If a patient feels that their sense of feeling a continuity of past, present, and future offers them a sense of security, is this to be interpreted as a defence or a sign of psychic health? If the patient's experience is predominantly one of gaps and discontinuities, does this indicate that s/he is "dissociated"? What are the implications of these different perspectives in relation to how the psychoanalyst views the possibilities and the experience of change?

A consideration of the notion of "forgetting" highlights some of the problems and paradoxes involved in the question of the subject's continuity. In his presentation of the analysis of Regular Zürcher, the existential psychoanalyst, Boss, includes an extract of a letter in which she appreciatively describes how, towards the end of the psychoanalytic work, she had begun to think of herself "more and more outright as a *woman without a past* or earlier life" (Boss, 1979, p. 17). In Boss's account he conveys how, at the beginning, Zürcher's memories had been exceedingly intense and overwhelming, and he stresses that the analyst's "steadiness" through this time, during which her extensive psychosomatic symptoms disappeared, was crucial. Boss does not comment on the connection between Zürcher's recollections of her past and the amelioration of her symptoms. I suspect that Zürcher's memories or stories about her past were important in enabling this particular shift but I think that her pleasure at now being a *"woman without a past"* deserves reflection.

Although more dramatically conceptualised, Zürcher's words resonate with those of my patient, Laura, who said to me after many years in analysis that she sometimes tried to remember the times when she had been treated abusively by men "but the memories are fading. I feel more distant from them". The relief she felt from this was very evident, but she was also wondering whether this meant that they were once again repressed. It felt to me that it was appropriate that these memories were receding. Our earlier work had been important in enabling Laura to remember and/or construct these memories or experiences in order for their power over her to diminish.

Freud's theorizing unrealistically emphasizes the importance of a *complete* remembering of that which is repressed, resisted, and defended against, denied or dissociated from. Lacan claims (but does not expand on) that in analysis there is an aim integral to this remembering: the patient is encouraged to remember in order to be able to forget. As Ricoeur reminds us, "the specter of a memory that would never forget anything ... we ... consider ... to be monstrous" (Ricoeur, 2004, p. 413). However, as the examples above indicate, it is important to consider what this "forgetting" entails.

Dosse, the contemporary French historian, argues against a notion of continuous history but he is also concerned with the "duty of memory" which, he argues, must be preceded by the "work of memory" (Dosse, 2006, p. 79). For example, if the extreme and extensive suffering experienced by the Jews at the time of the holocaust is forgotten, we cannot, as Ricoeur emphasizes, protect the future from the errors of the past. This duty of memory extends beyond oneself to others. However, a certain "forgetting" is necessary in order not to be "held captive by unhappiness" (Dosse, 2006, p. 82), which is what Bosse's and my own patient are referring to (see above). In response to this problem Ricoeur theorizes an "oubli" (a "forgotten"), which is a "memory-as-care" (Ricoeur, 2004, p. 505) available for recall as "what has been". Ricoeur conceptualizes this as "Carefree memory on the horizon of concerned memory, the soul common to memory that forgets and does not forget" (Ricoeur, 2004, p. 505).

The work of psychoanalysis is, in part, a project of remembering in order to release the individual from the compulsive hold of unconscious memories. When these memories recede, finding their place in the individual's past, they are nevertheless accessible to a re-remembering which allows them to be, consciously and unconsciously, creatively learnt from and reshaped, according to different contexts, opening out a different relation to the future. This neither relies on a concept of time as linear nor of a unified subject containing an internal store of memories; it is a dynamic process.

The importance of resisting notions of analysis which claim to enable the patient to discover or construct a solid unified self is argued for by Flax. Such an aim is bound to be disappointed since, according to Flax, in line with much post-modernist thought from Lyotard on, the subject is "a shifting and always changing intersection of complex, contradictory, and unfinished processes" (Flax, 1993, p. 108). The temporality of subjectivity is implied in her account of the subject as always changing. She argues that the illusion of a unified self relies on "relations of domination", namely dissociation from, or repression or control of, other aspects of one's own and other individuals' subjectivities. Resistance to domination, politically and personally, requires instead "multiple and fluid subjects" (Flax, 1993, p. 110) and the recognition of these as contextual.

Laing, by contrast, describes the precariousness of individuals in schizoid states who do not feel embodied (which he views as the foundation for a sense of continuity) and live with the constant threat of "attack, mutilation, disease, decay, and death" (Laing, 1961, p. 67). A person in a psychotic state may be so unable to assume a continuity of being in time to the extent that, for example, he loses any sense of himself as the agent of his own perceptions, believing that someone else is using his eyes and ears. However Laing also acknowledges that subjects exist "between being and non-being" (Laing, 1961, p. 51), and that non-being does not necessarily carry the threat of disintegration. The ability to be absorbed in listening to music or other creative activities requires an ability to tolerate a state of non-being which, he argues, is integral to human subjects as finite. Although Hoffman's (1989) position appears closer to Flax's, her subtle differentiation between being "split" by the differences between Polish and English and moving between them resonates with Laing's distinctions.

Tom Ryan, a relational psychoanalyst, poses the possibility of a "fine balance" between the experience of an "illusory", constant, continuous self and the experience of a less conscious, discontinuous, changeable self" (Ryan, 2004, p. 154). He compares the relational worlds of two women living in a therapeutic community (these could be described as world-designs in Binswanger's terms). One of the women relies on maintaining a rigid and unchanging perception of herself as needy and deprived (sometimes through various somatic complaints) to ward off her fears of disintegration. The other woman's relationships are characterised by (con)fusion, indecision, and lack of separateness. Tom Ryan alerts us to the dangers of either a too rigid or a too fragmented self identity which, although he does not say it explicitly, both cut the individuals off from their future.

The subtle differentiations between different states of being and non-being, of continuity and discontinuity in time, some of which productively opened out future possibilities and some of which were limiting were vividly conveyed to me by my patient, Owen. In one session he said to me that he frequently felt he was "somewhere else". He struggled to articulate how this felt, saying to me, "you may have experienced this in reading". He described shifting imperceptibly from an awareness of the act of reading into being absorbed by a reality which is very different and extremely far away from one's own (usual) reality. Owen then went on to clarify that what really concerned him were states in which it was "more like gazing at landscapes through a train window". Emerging from them, he was unable to recall any of them" knowing only that he had been "elsewhere", completely absent in someone else's presence. These states seemed to him to be "timeless". He thought this happened when there are tensions or conflicts in his relationship with another person.

For Owen, it seemed that these breaks in the continuity of his (usual) being served different functions. Complete absorption in reading enabled Owen to imaginatively live in and be affected by the world offered by the book. For Owen, the state he was specifically concerned about occurred at times other than reading. In our discussion it emerged that this particular "not being there" was an unconscious movement away from others into a time which was unreachable by others. He realized that he had developed this early on in his childhood, growing up without any private space of his own and so rarely any time on his own. When the time of others threatened to consume him he drifted away into another time, the events of which he did not remember on his "return". This posed a particular problem for him as an adult as it prevented him from acting in the world he shared with others, from changing or challenging what felt difficult or frustrating for him.

My work with Owen raises the question as to the problem of normative or universalizing assumptions regarding the time of the subject. In my work with Owen the discontinuity in his sense of identity was, at times, useful and at other times restrictive. Sometimes it opened out possibilities for the future, sometimes it fixed him in the present. His disappearance into a different time provided an important means of survival for him in his childhood. It had now, however, become problematic to him, hindering his ability to make life changes that he later came to see as necessary for him. His ability to absorb himself in reading was important to him: he loved language and he soon began, in his analysis, to experiment with writing (an interest he had had as a very young man). This became a way to reflect on his relationships with other people and on future directions in his own life. His absorption in the activity of writing opened out the possibility of his taking action in relation to the future. It was my attentiveness to his descriptions in language of the precise differences in these states of non-being which was critical to my understanding of them.

Timeless absorption

The absorption required for creative activities deserves greater attention in psychoanalytic practices, particularly since, for many individuals, the inability to "concentrate" (as it is often described) can be a particularly debilitating aspect of their suffering. The importance of absorption is recognized in Jung's and Winnicott's theorizing of creativity and also in Freud's concept of "evenly-suspended attention" (Freud, 1912e, p. 111). Freud develops this with his warning to the analyst not to take notes during or after sessions as this may interfere with the spontaneous emergence of the analyst's unconscious associations in the state of suspended attention. Bion (1970) takes this further in strongly advocating that the analyst approaches sessions without memory in order to be more fully attuned to what arises in the present between the analyst and the patient.

Classical descriptions of absorption as a state of "eternity" or "transcendence", with their religious or English Romantic associations have resulted in the assumption that this state is of another era or another realm and not relevant contemporaneously or compatible with the speed and immediacy of our technological culture. However, it is precisely because of its neglect in Western contemporary culture that we need to open out conceptualisations of it.

As Owen described in relation to his reading and, later, his writing, many individuals experience creative absorption as "timeless". In this state we are not conscious of time passing in any quantifiable, chronological or linear way. We are, as Rickman describes, "lost in what we are doing, caught up completely in the 'now', ... you are the music while the music lasts" (Rickman, 1964, p. 192). This absorption does not necessarily require solitude; it can be experienced in intimacy with another or others. The ability to experience this depends on being able to relinquish attention to everything other than what is being focused on in the present. In the case of writing or producing work which we want others to see or hear, we simultaneously include in our absorbed attention a relation to an other or imaginary other.

Absorption, if it is to be productive, requires a relaxing of self-protectiveness ("defences") and an openness to the "otherness" of what might emerge, particularly the "otherness" of unconscious thoughts and feelings (one's own and others' if they are present with us). These thoughts are often the source of originality and, as Jung and Winnicott indicate (see Ellis, 2008), point towards the future and they do not always appear to us in any linear sequence. Assumptions that the "timelessness" of absorption is necessarily reminiscent of the early undifferentiated mother infant relationship, such as Sabbadini (1989) implies, do not allow for the way in which absorption can involve an opening out to the otherness of the other. Freud's notion of "evenly-suspended attention" (Freud, 1912e, p. 111), which he regards as essential to effective listening on the part of the analyst does, in contrast, crucially constitute such an openness.

For some individuals such profound immersion in one activity may be associated with loss of control and with vulnerability. For others, the interruption in their sense of identity as continuous in time, or the possibility of being "at one" with an activity, or with another, can feel too threatening. If the analyst is sufficiently able to be absorbed by the experiences as conveyed through the patient's language, whether verbal or non-verbal, the specific meanings of, and associations to, these states of timelessness and their significance for the individual's creativity will emerge.

Time and the other

The phenomenological method of attending to the descriptions of a person's lived experiences enables us to expand traditional psychoanalytic analyses of lived time. Owen's descriptions of states of disappearing into another time and my subsequent reflections on creative forms of absorption raise the question as to how far we ever share the same time as others. According to Merleau-Ponty, individuals' temporalities are not entirely separate "because each one knows itself only by projecting itself into the present where they can interweave" (Merleau-Ponty, 1962, p. 433). Our present opens back into our past, forward into our future, and towards the temporalities of others of which we become a part and take forward in our lives. In contrast, Levinas, who worked contemporaneously with

Merleau-Ponty in Paris, argues in his theorizing of temporality that the subject and the Other never share the same time.

As we have seen in Chapter Four Levinas uses the term "the Other" for the other person whom one encounters in the "face-to-face" relationship. In contrast to Heidegger's theorizing of the "mineness" of death (see above), Levinas argues that what is crucial about our relation to our death is that it allows us to be *in relation to* that which is absolutely Other; in recognizing the unknowability of death, we realize the otherness of the Other. The Other is, like Death, ungraspable and ultimately mysterious to us: "the Other is what I myself am not" (Levinas, 1947b, p. 83). Furthermore our awareness of the mortality of the face of the Other demands of us a responsibility to them, requiring us to be neither an accomplice to, nor indifferent to, their death. This responsibility does not rely on reciprocity. For Levinas, writing within his Talmudic interpretation of his Jewish tradition, it is "for-the-other-person" (Levinas, 1947b, p. 137) and it is an openness to beyond being, to God and to infinity.

The Other's time disrupts my own and the Other as "future" reveals to me my relationship with the future. Our temporality is therefore intrinsically intersubjective. This is emphasized in Levinas's analysis of the caress as not knowing what it seeks in touching, as opening out what is ungraspable: "The caress is the anticipation of this pure future [*avenir*] without content" (Levinas, 1947b, p. 89). He connects avenir (French for "the future") and a venir (French for "to come"). He contrasts this notion of the erotic with Freud's theorizing of the libido as searching for a definite "content" or "fact", namely pleasure. For Levinas what is intrinsic to sexual intimacy is the search for the mysterious. Levinas's notion of the relation with the Other as being a relation with the future also contrasts strongly with Lacan's notion of the third term (the law of the Father) as necessarily disrupting the fusion of the early mother-infant relationship. For Levinas, the relation with the other contains an absence which is time itself and he argues against such a notion of an "intermediary" (Levinas, 1947b, p. 94) or of alterity as spatially differentiated (Levinas, 1947b, p. 84).

Levinas's challenge to the idea that the erotic relation is one of fusion is original. However, surprisingly, he argues that it is in the feminine that the dimension of alterity appears. This does assume a heterosexual intimacy and, in order to understand this, it is important to take into account the particular socio-historical context in which Levinas was writing. Although (as he acknowledges), feminists at this time were already voicing their demands for equality with men, within the field of philosophy, his recognition of gender difference (in contrast to notions of the generic "man" or the sexually neutral Dasein) was a radical move as a philosopher. Furthermore, despite the stereotype implied in his equation of the feminine with the mysterious, Levinas's view of the feminine as Other does not designate her as subordinate to the masculine as De Beauvoir (1949) wrongly assumes. He prioritizes her as the Other that is not possessable and cannot be encompassed by the Same. O'Connor's feminist reading of Levinas emphasizes that "The otherness of the feminine cuts through the self's egoistic self-inherence ... (allowing us to) begin 'to think' the possibility of voluptuosity which does not exclude the social, the practice of differences." (O'Connor, 1988, p. 67).

Levinas's view of the instant as an original moment which disrupts continuity contrasts with Merleau-Ponty's notion of identity as continuous through time, identified with time. Like Merleau-Ponty, Levinas challenges the classical Greek (Aristotelian) abstract representational view of time as linear, spreading from past to future, with separate instants, as inert measurements of time, placed between. However, he retains the notion of instants as separate. They are, for Levinas, insubordinate to time as a whole and interrupt its duration. They are a "beginning, a birth" (Levinas, 1947a, p. 76) and they are constituted by both evanescence (fading) and expectation. They therefore do not in themselves have duration. In each instant what is absolute is the materiality of the relationship between the subject's mastery of existence and the weight of concrete existence bearing down on the subject. This materiality is derived from the present. Each instant is "like a breathlessness, a panting, an effort to be" (Levinas, 1947a, p. 79). This resonates with Hoffman's conclusion in her very last sentence in Lost in Translation: "Time pulses through my blood like a river. The language of this is sufficient. I am here now" (Hoffman, 1989, p. 280). According to Levinas, engagement with the world depends on the evanescence of the instant and the presence of the present bestows an appearance of being to the past and "defies" the future which cannot eradicate it. It is nevertheless free of the past; as "the occurrence of an origin", the present "turns into a being" (Levinas, 1947a, p. 79). What is crucial about the instant, moreover, is its *"stance"* (Levinas, 1947a, p. 77). By this Levinas means that the instant enables the subject to "take a position" (Levinas, 1947a, p. 81) towards the world, thereby coming into existence. (See O'Connor, Chapter Ten, for more discussion of this.)

For psychoanalytic practices which are concerned with a sensitivity to the uniqueness of the patient's experience Levinas's view of the Other as absolutely other is an important contribution. Otherness, as theorized by Levinas, exceeds rational understanding, a gathering into the "same" and requires an originality of response to the patient which allows for those individual possibilities that escape over-arching theories. The universalism claimed for many psychoanalytic theories does not allow for the irreducible otherness of individuals. It contributes to the possibility of this being feared, ignored or denied by the psychoanalyst who is in flight from their own, and the patient's, anxiety and confusion regarding the limits of knowledge and understanding. The critical importance of this is highlighted in working with people from cultural and religious backgrounds, ages, and sexualities which may differ considerably from the analyst's own. Levinas's theorizing reminds the analyst of the importance of their responsibility in relation to the specificity of the patient's experience as always beyond their own. This does not mean it cannot be responded to, but it requires us to be attentive to the limits of empathy, with its implicit assumption that the psychoanalyst feels exactly the *same* as the patient.

Individuals' relations to time vary considerably between cultures and are shaped by cultural and religious traditions (for example, specific perspectives on death and immortality, understandings of history, the role of memory and narrative), work patterns, the climate, and the length of daylight time as well as many other factors. In psychoanalytic work with couples the differences in individuals' relation to time are particularly highlighted. For one couple it was a relief for them to identify how one of them always lived in anticipation of the future, planning for every eventuality, including the possibility (or likelihood) of death. The other was unafraid of death and lived more in the immediacy of the present, often feeling at risk of being consumed by others' demands which she felt she had to respond to immediately.

Levinas's notion that the Other is always in a different time is very relevant to the relation between patient and analyst. Although they both agree on the frequency and duration of the session in clock time (except in Lacanian psychoanalysis where sessions are of a variable length) the lived time of the session is not however shared (Green, 2002). In their speaking and their gestures, in the rhythms, gaps, unconscious slips and silences, both the psychoanalyst and the patient weave in and out of different times, between their pasts, presents and possible futures. Moreover, the difference between the times of the participants is itself critical to the psychoanalytic work. When, for the patient, the future closes down under the shadow of despair, the analyst must both remain alive to its possibilities, and also responsive to the drudgery of endless suffering. In listening to the dread of what may happen in the future, the analyst may turn her/his attention to the patient's past. Incidents in previous sessions, memories recalled and reforgotten by the patient, each with their own horizons, seize the analyst's attention together with the personal associations which may elucidate or obscure the otherness of the patient's experiences.

In the patient's transferences past experiences may be lived as present with their "pastness" torn from them and their difference from the present precluded from consciousness. The transference may also be a form of experimenting with new possibilities of relationships, pointing towards the future. The newness of the instant as theorized by Levinas is the promise of the opportunity for change in psychoanalysis. The appearance of an instant in which the past cannot be present and where the future does not yet exist offers the possibility of the taking up of a new position, of breaking the compulsion to attempt to repeat that which, in fact, can never be repeated. This taking up of a new position occurs in the relationship between the psychoanalyst and the patient, in the difference between them, in the time that points towards the future. It is an original unrepeatable instant in which both individuals are changed, consciously and/or unconsciously. The new position is a creation that is born between them and, in its freedom, it carries paradoxically, the weight of responsibility to oneself and to others.

Conclusion

The work of Heideggger, Merleau-Ponty, Foucault and Levinas enhances the possibilities for psychoanalytic practices which are more sensitive to individuals' experiences of time. As I indicate at the beginning of the chapter, I do not claim that any one of these positions is more relevant than another nor that there is one "mature" perspective on time for which psychoanalytic practices must aim. Through their diverse positions, the analyst is alerted to the importance of an attentiveness to the dominance of particular time dimensions in individuals' speech, their relation to these dimensions and to others' time, and to whether and how these temporal experiences are sources of conflict and suffering and/or of hope. Similarly, the specificity of *how* individuals experience their identities, whether as punctuated with gaps or as continuous through time, must not be assumed to be *in itself* productive or problematic for the individual in psychoanalysis. This differs for different individuals at different times.

CHAPTER EIGHT

Images of sexualities; Language and embodiment in art therapy

Mary Lynne Ellis

Introduction

My aim in this chapter is to generate further discussion as to how we can more sensitively address questions of sex and sexualities in art therapy. There is a surprising dearth of theorizing within art therapeutic literature in relation to these issues. This may arise from the strong strand of individualism in the art profession that appears to allow for sexual freedom; subsequently, it is supposed perhaps that there is nothing problematic to discuss. Alternatively, there may an assumption that psychoanalytic theory with its proliferation of discourses on sexuality can offer us all we require. This chapter challenges such assumptions.

Sexualities and sexual identities emerge in diverse ways and hold more or less importance at different times in individuals' lives. They are not fixed and they may be the source of and constructed through a multiplicity of complex experiences within specific social contexts. Classical psychoanalytic theorizing, in contrast, continues to conceive of sexuality in terms of early developmental stages, claiming that heterosexuality is more "natural" or "healthy" than lesbian, gay or bisexual sexualities. In challenging this view

121

I emphasize the importance in art therapy of attending to the unique meanings which are associated with sexuality for each individual. I reflect on how of the theorizing of modern European philosophers such as Merleau-Ponty can enable art therapists to be more alive to the diversity of languages of sexualities. Furthermore I argue that the medium of art in psychotherapy can offer a particularly valuable language for exploration of the theme of sex and sexualities in the art therapeutic relationship.

Questions of sexuality in art therapy

In the introduction to his book *The Sexual Perspective, Homosexuality and Art in the Last Hundred Years in the West*, a thorough and comprehensive documentation of the lives and practices of artists who have defined themselves as homosexual, or had significant relationships with people of the same sex, Cooper, the gay art critic, suggests that the art profession has

> traditionally offered homosexuals an outlet for their sensitivity, a place where, however limited, some expression of their sexuality can be made without fear of ridicule or dismissal, a relatively safe community within which some sort of identity may be established (Cooper, 1986, p. xv).

His words point to a number of issues that are pertinent to the question of why the theme of sex and sexualities has been so little addressed in art therapeutic literature and, simultaneously, how the art therapeutic relationship might offer a particularly valuable context for the exploration of sexuality. Although the liberal individualism of many artistic communities has contributed to a greater acceptance of diverse sexualities than exists in many other communities, it has, at the same time, tended to deny the wider political significance of individuals' styles of living. The question for art therapists is how we can offer a reflective space that allows for exploration of different sexualities and which also recognizes the particular socio-cultural and socio-historical contexts within which identities are lived. This includes developing a sensitivity to the specific effects on the individual of particular forms of discrimination.

A further difficulty for psychotherapists (whether art or verbal) in addressing the question of sexuality is the awareness of the intimacy and complexity of the analytical relationship. In my experience of both training and supervising art therapists and psychotherapists many of them have admitted fears regarding erotic transference and counter-transference: these have ranged from anxieties that there might be a temptation for the therapist to become sexually involved with a patient to fears of not being sensitive enough to the patient's vulnerability in their exploration of sexual desire in their therapy. These are understandable fears given the historical and cultural context in which we work. Schaverien's inspiring discussion of these themes in *Desire and the Female Therapist* is reassuring in the face of such fears. She emphasizes that "the emergence of eros, which is generated in the transference ... is purposeful. It is a sign of life and a move towards individuation for therapist as well as patient" (Schaverien, 1995, p. xi). If we are open to the theme of sexuality, we are alert to the possibilities of aliveness in the patient. This is demonstrated in Schaverien's case studies where her sensitive and creative use of the erotic transference emerges as highly transformative in the therapeutic relationship.

Throughout her book Schaverien, as a feminist, acknowledges the importance of the socio-cultural in shaping relationships between people "of whatever gender" (Schaverien, 1995, p. 28). The role of the social context in the construction of gender is the focus of Hogan's (1997) collection, *Feminist Approaches to Art Therapy*. The contributors address a diverse range of themes relevant to women's identities, which include feminist theories of development, breast cancer, pregnancy, race, embodiment, aging and motherhood and others. It is an important contribution to the growing body of literature in art therapy which acknowledges the cultural and historical specificity of experiences and challenges normative notions of subjectivity.

The book contains many sensitive descriptions of how women's experiences of their sexuality have emerged in art therapy in relation to aging (Huet), an art therapist's pregnancy (Skaife), and sexuality and motherhood (Hogan). Their work is a crucial reminder that heterosexuality takes multifarious forms according to the context. It is surprising, in the light of this, that there are scarcely any references in this volume to lesbian, gay, and bisexual sexualities. Hogan's later book, *Gender Issues in Art Therapy* (2003), redresses this in its inclusion of three chapters by Addison, Fraser and Waldman, and de Oliveira which reflect specifically on questions of lesbian, gay, bisexual and transgendered experiences in relation to art therapy provision and practices. Their chapters are important contributions to the development of critical thinking in relation to how art therapists might address questions of sexual identities and homophobia.

In this chapter, I focus particularly on lesbian, gay, and bisexual sexualities. This is not to assume that any identities, including heterosexual ones, are fixed or imply any predictable styles of being. Furthermore, my reflections on the relation between sexualities and language is equally relevant to all sexualities. Throughout, I emphasize that sexualities do not exist outside specific cultural, historical, and linguistic contexts.

Am I a Lesbian?

In order to introduce my own perspective on working with questions of sexuality in art therapy I present some vignettes from a one-day therapy workshop I ran entitled "Am I a Lesbian?". The identities of the women are, of course, disguised to preserve their confidentiality. This workshop was one of a number of theme-centred weekend therapy workshops on offer in an annual programme in a women's centre. The women came to the workshop in the hope that they might achieve some certainty about their sexual orientation. For some women this was conceptualised as finding their "real" selves as lesbian or straight, one or the other. As facilitator I structured the day to include discussion in pairs, in small groups, and in the large group, as well as using art therapy at the beginning of the day.

The discussion which developed amongst the women throughout the day was important as a source of support for them as they struggled with their anxiety and uncertainty and also with the possible consequences of making certain choices in their lives in relation to their sexuality. They knew that if they did choose to identify as lesbian they would also have to find the strength to deal with the likelihood of homophobic responses as well as major life changes, including possible losses of close relationships. Through my interventions I aimed to open out the more unconscious aspects of their questions and exploration as well as identifying some of the similarities and the differences in their experiences. However, the images that the women created were particularly powerful for them as very vivid reflections of the individuality, complexity, and possibilities of their sexualities which they returned to at many points during the day.

It was after the women had verbally introduced themselves to one another in turns, that I invited them to use art materials to address the question, "What is your experience of your sexuality now?". The atmosphere in the room as the women worked on their images was one of intense anxiety, hesitation, and excitement. In the group discussion which followed, Anna said that she had struggled with trying to press her piece of clay into shape and that she realized "how much I have tried to do this with my sexuality". Seeing the marks that the clay had left on the paper beneath it, she had drawn into them, excited at the idea that similarly her sexuality could, in her words, "emerge or happen, without having to be pushed into a definite shape". Another participant, Sandra, had swept crayon marks into a curving crest which, she told the group, was "like an orgasm". Next to it a small field of scarlet poppies had appeared. She said she was amazed at the intensity of their colour, yet they were contained in such a small space. Sandra felt these poppies expressed for her "the joy I have had to deprive myself of for so long". An area of crayoning, merging and fluid was "a solid part, the possibility of meeting another woman sexually". She tentatively wondered how she would be able to manage the double stigmatisation of being lesbian and being black and "the shame I might feel". Belinda's tiny clay figure curved over in the yoga position, "pose of a child", hid her face from an angry mother. As she spoke in the group she realized that "to be intimate with a man or a woman will never be possible while I am so fearful of my mother". Lucy associated her black and purple scribbles, which surrounded a glowing red patch encircled by a protective line, with her "sadness and confusion; there have been too many relationships with men that have disappointed me, yet I am terrified of being with a woman".

Through their artwork the women in the group discovered an embodying language for their ambiguity and uncertainty and, through describing their imagery, they found new words and new speech. They were able to begin to acknowledge the importance of the individuality of their own socio-culturally specific sexualities and to consider how they might find the courage to assert these.

There was discussion as to the relation between these and different possible identities, for example, being lesbian, being black, being bisexual, being a woman, being a mother, or having a work or professional identity. Anna's attempts to push her clay into shape gave rise to the question of whether sexualities are ever fixed and whether they can be consciously chosen.

The women's work crystallized so vividly how diverse experiences of sexuality are and how important it is for art and verbal psychotherapists/analysts to develop a perspective which is attentive to the specificity of individuals' sexualities as they emerge within particular relational contexts (including gender, race, class and the myriad of others). Furthermore this attentiveness relies on a recognition of the critical importance of language in therapeutic practices. The language of the women's visual (and tactile imagery) and the verbal interpretations which unfolded from these highlighted the distinctiveness and poetry of their particular sexual worlds.

Alienating interpretations

The uniqueness of patients' language for their sexualities is often not attended to in classical psychoanalystic accounts. As Noreen O'Connor and Joanna Ryan (1993) argue in their rigorously researched and challenging book *Wild Desires and Mistaken Identities, Lesbianism and Psychoanalysis,* these analysts' theorizing tends to be based on a very few individual cases and on much cross-referencing between writers. Furthermore, as Noreen O'Connor and Joanna Ryan also point out, while claiming that their theories are based on observation and are value-free, their theorizing is underpinned by a fundamental assumption that homosexuality and lesbianism are psychopathologies. Masud Khan's account of his work (in *Alienation in Perversions*) with a woman patient who is in an intimate relationship with another woman starkly exemplifies such an assumption and highlights how little he is concerned with the specificity of the patient's own language.

Khan coldly reports a woman patient's experience of sex with another woman: "she now recounted how she liked licking the grooves round the neck of her friend, it always gave her an uncanny feeling of her friend's wholeness and smoothness. *The impulse to eat and bite was only thinly veiled here. The fight with the oral-sadistic and the anal-sadistic impulses now came to the fore"* (Khan, 1964, p. 91) He claims "the tongue ... was fantasised as the castrated genital. It had a restitutive role both in relation to the object and the self body ego ... in so far as it symbolized the penis it made good to her partner what she had been deprived of in being taken away from her male lover (father)" (1964, p. 85).

From the few words of this woman regarding her pleasure with her partner (Khan does not produce any further associations from her in her own speech), Khan pronounces the "truth" about her same-sex sexuality: it is a defence against destructive impulses, it restores, in phantasy, a fragmented body-ego, and also the destroyed "object", and it is an attempt to heal the loss of the father's penis. For Khan, there can be no sex without a penis somewhere.

The contrast between the language of this psychoanalyst (his patient is denied her own language) and the language of the women in the workshop, both visual and spoken, jolts us. Khan's is the voice of certainty, of pathology, (homosexuality in women and men can only be symptomatic of this), of destruction and defences, of universality (all women desire the penis and have to acknowledge their own castration) and of developmental failure. Furthermore his position is underpinned by a Cartesian notion of the subject: the external body's behaviour with its "impulses" is driven by the dynamics of internal psychic forces.

Khan's account is just one example of numerous classical psychoanalytic theories pathologizing homosexuality which have emerged from Freudian, Kleinian, post Object Relations, Jungian, and Lacanian strands (see Noreen O'Connor and Joanna Ryan's (1993) comprehensive analysis of these). The "cause" of homosexuality is attributed to fixations at the pre-Oedipal and Oedipal stages and it is variously interpreted as a narcissistic condition, a defence against envy at the breast, psychosis, the fear of disintegration and mutilation amongst numerous other possibilities. The Oedipus complex is still assumed in these theories to be universal, regardless of the particular socio-historical or socio-cultural context in which an individual is raised. Since the "normal" outcome of the Oedipus complex is the taking up of a heterosexual position, there is no place within such theories for notions of lesbian, gay and bisexual sexualities as mature, creative, healthy, or loving. As O'Connor and Ryan point out, the unreflective rigidity of classical psychoanalytic accounts of sexuality contradicts the very radical aspects of its interpretations of human subjectivity. Such theorizing has also led to the exclusion of lesbians and gay men from psychoanalytic trainings in Britain until recently (see Ellis, 1994 and Twomey, 2003).

Transforming psychoanalysis

Although, in this chapter, I am addressing the limitations of classical psychoanalytic theorising of sexuality I want to emphasise that my critique does not undermine for me the importance of many of its basic tenets: its recognition of the limits of rationality in human subjectivity, its engagement with those aspects of our experiences of which we are unconscious, and its acknowledgement of the significance of our histories and of the critical importance of the transferential relationship. Enrooted in these tenets are the concepts of identification, projection, splitting, resistance, dissocciation, displacement, all of which, together with many others, I find useful in understanding the texture of my patients' worlds, including their relationship with me.

It is important to emphasize that all of these conscious and unconscious aspects of relating take place in language. In "language" I include the spoken, gestural, and visual (in the form of metaphors and dreams) since, of course, even where visual imagery is not specifically encouraged as in art psychotherapy, it is manifest throughout all of our discourses. If we attend sensitively to the specificity of patients" languages and suspend any desire to generalize or universalise we can allow questions to emerge for us which might address the complexity of each individual's experience more fully. The language of our responses to the patient may be informed by particular concepts from psychoanalytic theory (or literature, other art forms, and philosophy) but I think that it is crucial to regard these as contingent metaphors which can sensitively meet, crystallize, or open out a patient's experience.

Furthermore, our responses arise from the intersubjectivity of my our relationships with each individual patient in its specific context. The patient and I both bring to this our past, our present, and our anticipation of the future, and our multiple conscious and unconscious identities, (albeit not always articulated by the therapist), and we are both affected by what occurs. In the language between patient and therapist past experiences of relationships re-emerge (although never exactly as before) and new possibilities are explored. The transference is, as Freud writes, and Schaverien's theorizing of the erotic demonstrates, a "playground" (Freud, 1914 g, p. 154) for these explorations.

Although I set a theme for the women in the workshop to address through their artwork, this is not my usual approach in my ongoing analytic art and verbal psychotherapy work. However, my attention to the women's own descriptions of their experiences and to their particular conscious and unconscious experiences of their embodiment is characteristic of my perspective which is, as I discuss below, influenced by Merleau-Ponty's phenomenological approach. My focus was on the specific relations between their experiences of joy, fear, playfulness, loss, sadness, and excitement, the reasons or purpose for their confusion, the connection between this and the socio-historical and cultural expectations of certainty in relation to sexual identity and orientation, the manifestation of their experiences as sometimes simultaneous, sometimes split, sometimes shifting, the relation between their present and their past, and also their experimentation with future possibilities of their sexualities. My concern was not with why they had sexual desires for other women (the classical psychoanalytic position) but, rather, what their conscious and unconscious experiences of their desires were.

Phenomenology

Phenomenology's importance to psychoanalytic practices has been argued for by existential psychoanalysts such as Binswanger and Boss as early as the 1930s and, more recently, in the 1960s, by R.D. Laing. As a philosophical method, phenomenology was founded by the German philosopher, Husserl (1859–1938), a student of Franz Brentano's in Vienna, who also taught Freud. It aims to investigate phenomena as they appear in human consciousness. Its primary emphasis is on attending to the specificity of our *descriptions* of states of being rather than explanations of experience in terms of causes (See also Chapters Five and Seven). In the examples above, Khan's analysis is concerned with the *cause* of the woman's homosexuality, while my response in relation to the women's artwork and their speech was one of engagement with the specificity of their descriptions of their sexualities in relation to the context, including myself and the other group members.

Phenomenological texts are concerned with the everyday world of human existence. They emphasise the temporality of the human subject and are concerned with descriptions of states of being in relation to oneself and to others, such as anxiety, the anticipation of death, love, desire and sexuality. These are, of course, concerns that many people bring to art therapy and verbal psychotherapy. For phenomenologists the meaning of experience is crucial and they argue against the idea that we can possess a complete understanding of our own origins since, from birth, we are thrown into an already constituted world of language, of family constellations, and our culture. This contrasts with Freud's emphasis on the analyst acquiring a "complete" picture of everything the patient has repressed (Freud, 1937, p. 256). A phenomenological perspective holds that such understanding is always only partial and disclosure of existence always depends on the context.

This context is always intersubjective and linguistic (verbally and non-verbally). We are always already in a world of others, whether in the presence or absence of them. For Heidegger it is our "intonation, modulation, tempo and 'the way of speaking'" (Heidegger, 1962, pp. 204–206) which is most crucial: language is *between* people. Both art therapists and analysts are consciously and unconsciously responding to these aspects of language between ourselves and our patients and they are integral to the transference and counter-transference relationship, yet the significance of them is rarely theorised.

Merleau-Ponty: Language and embodiment

The phenomenologist Merleau-Ponty (1962) takes this theorising further through his emphasis on the subject as embodied. As Skaife (2001) argues, his theorizing of embodiment and intersubjectivity is very relevant to art therapists. His work is interwoven throughout with references to painting, particularly Cezanne's work.

Merleau-Ponty argues that mind and body, subject and object, are not distinct and separate identities. We *are* our bodies and they are neither simply subjects nor objects, they are "our general medium for having a world" (Merleau-Ponty, 1962, p. 146). This constitutes a radical challenge to the dualistic thought (dating from Descartes), which permeates our Western culture, in which the individual is viewed as a body inhabited by a mind which steers it. From a phenomenological point of view, Anna's attempt to press her piece of clay into shape, as she said she felt she had done with her sexuality, could be interpreted as a reflection of our Western culture's mind-body split which she had absorbed through her past relationships and which impeded spontaneity in her sexuality. Such a split is not universally "given".

Merleau-Ponty's critique of the notion of the body and mind as separate and his analysis of the gestural aspects of painting lead him to theorize all language, including speech, as a form of gesture. He emphasizes that the picture, like the poem, novel, or musical work, is "a being in which the expression is indistinguishable from the thing expressed" (Merleau-Ponty, 1962, p. 151). Merleau-Ponty means that we do not represent a thought or feeling to ourselves internally and then express it. As Skaife explains, "The gesture made, for example, the brushstroke or the impression of the hand within the clay *is* the language, the expression, rather than being the translation of an idea or a thought. The making of the artwork, its facture, *is* its meaning" (my italics, Skaife, 2001, p. 46). This view of language informs Merleau-Ponty's challenge to the assumption that behaviour associated with, for example, anger or love is the same in all cultures: he argues that the difference of behaviour corresponds to a difference in the emotions themselves. His acknowledgement of the untranslatability of certain concepts and experiences is highly relevant to art therapeutic work with patients from cultural backgrounds very different to our own.

Sexuality, conscious/unconscious

Merleau-Ponty writes specifically about sexuality, arguing that it is "co-extensive with life" (Merleau-Ponty, 1962, p. 169). It is not a discrete realm of human experience and its source is not in any "autonomous reflex apparatus" (Merleau-Ponty, 1962, p. 155), i.e. biologically or anatomically based; the human subject is not "a bundle of instincts" (Merleau-Ponty, 1962, p. 166). While acknowledging Freud's contribution in showing that sexuality is what enables the subject to have a history, Merleau-Ponty makes an impassioned challenge against his naturalism: in designating certain orifices as eroticised in the pre-genital life of the infant Freud does not take into account the diverse possibilities for the developing child's sexual interest and how these arise from within particular socio-historical contexts. The oral, anal and genital stages are therefore not universal.

Merleau-Ponty theorizes a dialectical relationship between the body and existence. Sexuality is not an object of conscious intention; instead sexuality and existence are interfused, such that it not possible to designate an act or a decision "sexual or non-sexual" (Merleau-Ponty, 1962, p. 169). Sexuality is constantly present and it is ambiguous "like an atmosphere" (1962, p. 168); it "spreads forth like an odour or like a sound" (1962, p. 168). It is intersubjective and contextual, and therefore, historically and culturally specific. He describes it as being "diffused in images" (1962, p. 168) and this is revealed in dreams. The dream images are a form of language in which what is expressed is not distinct from its expression (see above). Merleau-Ponty thus emphasizes that we do not perceive something as genital and then translate it into figurative language: instead "the dreamer's penis *becomes* the serpent which appears in the manifest content" (Merleau-Ponty, 1962, p. 168). These are not distinct from one another. Merleau-Ponty problematises notions of the unconscious as a container, a discrete "inner" world completely distinct from consciousness and argues that, instead, like sexuality, it is co-extensive with life.

If we reflect on what occurred in the "Am I a Lesbian Workshop?" in the light of Merleau-Ponty's theorizing it is possible to see the relevance of his notion of sexuality and of the unconscious to art therapy practices. As a gestural language of touching, art making is a particularly valuable language for the exploration of sexualities. Art media are extensions of our embodied subjectivities. The images that emerge unconsciously through the hardness, fluidity, malleability, or softness of the art materials do not express inner representations of sexual drives; they are in themselves experiences of sexuality. In the same way, touching is not an external expression of an inner feeling of intimacy; touching *is* that intimacy.

Visual language also has a more extensive vocabulary. It allows for ambiguities, subtleties, and complexities more extensively than is possible in verbal language. This is particularly important when, given the taboos that have existed (and continue to exist in many cultures) against talking explicitly about sexualities, the words available to us are more limited. Additionally, since for the patient, talking about sexuality may feel embarrassing and exposing, particularly if there is eroticism in the transference, artwork may offer more safety for such exploration.

When Anna tried to press her clay into shape, she was not initially conscious of the relevance of this to her sexuality. At some point later, taking another perspective on her artwork in the context of the discussion in the group, she became conscious of this. Sandra's small field of bright poppies had appeared spontaneously, revealing what she had not been conscious of, namely how intense and yet how constrained her longing for intimacy with another woman was. Just as Merleau-Ponty writes of the dreamer's penis *becoming* the serpent, similarly, Sandra's sexuality *was*, at that moment, a small field of scarlet poppies. At another moment it had had the power of an ocean wave. It seemed that in confining her red poppies, Sandra was also unconsciously protecting herself; the force of the wave had felt liberating, but also shocking to her.

Anna's and Sandra's work in the group highlights the restrictions of a notion of the unconscious theorised as being entirely split from consciousness and from the wider social context. The ambiguity and complexity of the women's images cannot be adequately understood through notions of alinguistic, universal sexual impulses arising from within and subjected to repression. Merleau-Ponty's notions of sexuality and the unconscious as being "coextensive with life" (1962, p. 169) allow for more specific interpretations of an individual's experience at a particular moment, allowing its poetry and metaphors to speak.

If we assume that there is an "internal", psychological world as separate from an "external" world we do not adequately acknowledge how "in the world" our thoughts and actions are; it is just that we are not always conscious of *how* they are. I think that "conscious" and "unconscious" are thus useful adjectivally but not as nouns. Furthermore, as the women's exploration of their sexuality highlights, descriptions and associations arise out of shifting perspectives; as one view emerges, another recedes, depending on the context.

Sexualities in contexts

The images which emerged in the workshop were specific to the context. For example, for Sandra, the workshop was a place in which she felt secure enough to engage with the possibility, including her fears, of sexual pleasure with another woman. This feeling of safety can be viewed transferentially: Sandra created a relationship with both me as the therapist and also the group which allowed for honesty about her sexuality. It was not appropriate in the context of a one-day workshop to explore with her whether this arose from a relationship in her past, or was an experiment with a new one which could enable this, but I think these are both possibilities.

Sandra's relationship to myself and the group also allowed for the emergence of unconscious associations in relation to the expansiveness of the wave and the small size of the field. These referred specifically to the social contexts of black and white cultures in which, in her experience, same-sex sexuality was deemed abnormal and unacceptable. They were also connected with her mother's view of any overt sexuality in women as "cheap and dirty". All of these had contributed to her fears of (in her words) "standing out like a strange creature" as black and lesbian. I think that for Sandra, her exploration of the shame attached to her sexuality, was more possible in visual imagery than if she had had to rely primarily on words.

Schaverien's (1999) discussion of the value of art therapy for exploration of the impact of cultural attitudes and of cultural and racial stereotypes on body image is very relevant here. Focusing particularly on the experiences of Jewish people she emphasizes the power of racist characterisations of them in literature and art. Her account is reminiscent of the psychoanalyst Fanon's theorizing of how a black person's identity becomes embodied through the white other within a context of power relations in which s/he is, in his words, "woven … out of a thousand details, anecdotes, stories" (Fanon, 1952, p. 111) and designated as inferior. Fanon includes in his analysis the role of the media and of literature in shaping cultural identities. In a very vivid description he conveys the appalling bodily effects of being objectified in the face of a white child's fear of him as a black person so that "my body was given back to me sprawled out, distorted, recolored, clad in mourning on that white winter day ... the earth rasps under my feet, and there is a ... white song. All this whiteness that burns me" (Fanon, 1952, p. 113–114). In response to the racism of the white other, he decides to assert himself as a black man, to counter the irrationality of white racism. Refusing to conform to white culture he begins to identify with sensuality, with nature, with rhythm, and spontaneity. Yet he finds himself again stereotyped—as "primitive" (Fanon, 1952, p. 130).

Fanon draws on psychoanalytic theory in his analysis of racist assumptions that black people are more sexually potent than white people and argues that these are projections of their own desires. He also challenges the universality of the Oedipus complex (finding it to be absent in 97% of families in the French Antilles). As an anti-essentialist, he emphasises the differences *between* black people, challenging the notion of a "black psychology". He views his own task as freeing himself from his history, including that of slavery, from the dualisms of inferiority and superiority, "to touch the other, feel the other, to explain the other to myself" (Fanon, 1952, p. 231) and, above all, to never cease questioning.

Fanon's account resonates with Merleau-Ponty's accounts of embodiment as cultural but he goes further in including an analysis of the effects of racism. Unfortunately Fanon's theorizing of women's sexuality is limited by his surprising reliance on developmental theories which fail to acknowledge the social context of gender relations. However, his theorising of the role of power in the emergence of different black identities, which was extremely original at the time he wrote, converges somewhat with Foucault's regarding sexuality, yet pre-dates his by nearly twenty-five years.

For Foucault (although Fanon would not go as far as this), there is no body prior to history or to discourses; the body is totally imprinted by history and, moreover, *produced* by historical forces. He argues, as Fanon does in relation to race, that power is transmitted through discourses and practices relating to sexuality, producing culturally specific identities, including those arising as forms of resistance to a dominant discourse. The concept of "natural" as, for example, in the assumption that heterosexuality is more "natural" than homosexuality, is itself a social construct. For Foucault, the body is not a material or biological "fact". (See Chapter Two for more discussion of this). Noreen O'Connor and Joanna Ryan were innovative in drawing on Foucault's theorizing of the historical specificity of sexual identities for the development of a new psychoanalytic theorizing which does not assume that lesbianism is a pathology. They argue that

> It is, of course, fruitful to ask how far, and in what ways, struc-
> tures of oppression, which may be shared by many lesbians, do
> constitute or contribute to the forms of lesbian desire, but this is
> very different from perceiving inherent features of such desire
> (O'Connor & J. Ryan, 1993, p. 234).

The question of differences and the contingency of identities, how they shift and how they are interwoven, is central to Audre Lorde's (1982) novel *Zami*. *Zami* is a very rich account of a young black woman's life, beginning with her childhood in Harlem in the 1930s and extending through the 1950s and the McCarthy era. Lorde's language is vividly visual, tactile and sensual, and the novel highlights how same-sex love does not necessarily imply sameness in roles, identities, experiences, or cultures. Lorde is acutely sensitive to the socio-historical and cultural, including the linguistic contexts, of her characters, and her accounts of women making love with one another pose, as the women's paintings I described, a strong challenge to classical psychoanalytic accounts. Lorde never idealises the notion of identity; as a black lesbian she is very aware of the political necessity for identities and, at the same time, questions how these can also allow for individual differences. As I discuss in Chapter Two her theorising (in fictional form) is very relevant to analysts and art therapists working with questions of gender, race, and sexuality with their patients. I quote directly from her words as, in line with my emphasis on the importance of language, I want to retain their rhythms and their poetry:

> Being women together was not enough. We were different. Being
> gay-girls together was not enough. We were different. Being
> Black together was not enough. We were different. Being Black
> women together was not enough. We were different. Being
> Black dykes together was not enough. We were different (Lorde,
> 1982, p. 226).

Conclusion

Merleau-Ponty's, Foucault's, Fanon's and Lorde's theorising share an emphasis on the socio-historical specificity of embodied experiences and of sexual identities. This hinges on a view of language, whether verbal, gestural or visual, as creating worlds, rather than explaining an already existing world. Their work is particularly relevant to the art therapy relationship wherein possibilities are opened out through language; these are meaningful between the patient and the art therapist or analyst, but they are also contingent "truths" or perspectives which hold at a particular moment in time and which can shift over time to be replaced by new stories from fresh angles. For the art therapist attending to a patient's exploration of their sexuality the question should not, in my view, be *"what* is this individual's sexuality or sexual identity?" nor "what is the cause of it?" but "in what language or *how* are these being described, how intertwined or how distinct are they from a person's other identities or experiences? What are the particular conscious and unconscious meanings of them for this particular person in this particular context, including the effects on them of homophobia, racism, sexism? How might all of these be at play in the transference? How far, if at all, are any of my own identifications with any of these identities useful?" These questions are concerned with imaginatively addressing the uniqueness of each individual's experience, with differences, not universals. Above all, they are concerned with the crucial importance of the patient's own languages in their specificity, whether verbal, visual, gestural, or otherwise.

CHAPTER NINE

Homophobia is the patient

Mary Lynne Ellis

Introduction

The idea for this chapter arose one morning after seeing two patients consecutively. One was a young man of twenty-four who had had both heterosexual and gay relationships and who was now interested in having an intimate relationship with a man. However, he said, he "couldn't cope" with what identifying as gay might mean culturally. The other was a middle-aged woman who was continuing to feel periodically very troubled about her son identifying as gay and was expressing concern about her homophobia. The idea that a twenty-four year old young man who is generally not at all conventional in his thinking and in his life style is still terrified that at some point he might have to "come out" as gay and become the target of possibly considerable hostility because of loving another man, felt particularly shocking to me on that day: the huge achievements regarding sexual equality simultaneously sharply highlight how far the constraints on taking up these rights are still operative in people's day to day lives.

Noreen O'Connor and Joanna Ryan (1993) argue that pathologizing interpretations arise as defences against the anxieties aroused by working with lesbian and gay patients. They argue instead, as we do in this book, for recognition within psychoanalytic practices of the diversity of lesbian desires, socially, historically, and culturally. They challenge the notion of lesbian sexualities as sharing qualities in any essentialist sense. My reflections in this chapter similarly rest on a repudiation of any aim to "discover" a definitive explanation of homophobia, identifying its "causes" and "effects". To do this would be to risk replicating the approaches of those psychoanalytic theories which pathologize lesbianism and homosexuality, and fail to recognize their diversity. I also do not want to imply that homophobia is one thing or one process with one source; it manifests itself and functions in a multiplicity of ways and is more appropriately referred to in its plural form. Through my account of my work with my patient, Teresa, I critically reflect on a number of possible, not necessarily mutually exclusive, interpretations of what might constitute homophobia, or homophobias, drawing on the theories of Freud, Foucault, Butler and Levinas.

Reading Freud's homophobia

According to Freud, phobias are not "an independent pathological process" (Freud, 1909b, p. 115); they can appear as an aspect of many different forms of distress ranging across all the neuroses. He delineates three different groups of phobias:

1. phobias experienced by so-called "normal" people, such as fear of snakes. Freud claims that fears such as this are a "universal human characteristic" and they are therefore generally not accorded the status of "symptoms" or regarded as particularly troubling or inhibiting (Freud, 1916–1917, p. 399).
2. phobias of situations which are recognized by most people as entailing some risk, such as train travel, thunderstorms, crowds, enclosed spaces and solitude. Their status as phobias is related to the intensity of anxiety which anticipation of them evokes.
3. phobias which are, in Freud's words, "beyond our comprehension", such as animal phobias (Freud, 1916–1917, p. 399).

Some phobias, such as agoraphobia and fear of rail travel, are acquired later in life, while others, such as fear of the dark, of animals, and thunderstorms arise early on. However, all of the phobias relating to the second and third groups are, he argues, closely related to anxiety hysteria.

In "anxiety hysteria," according to Freud, phobias function as "defensive structures" against anxiety, which involve endless "precautions, inhibitions, or prohibitions" (Freud, 1909b, p. 117). He initially theorizes anxiety as arising in relation to an "internal threat" to the ego, such as libidinal or destructive impulses, rage, or shame. Freud later revises this to emphasize the significance of an "external" threat (Freud, 1926d, p. 126) and, in particular, the threat of castration. He retracts his previous assumption that anxiety arises from repressed libido and argues that anxiety has its source in the attitude of the ego. It is the anxious ego which initiates repression.

In his analysis of the case of Little Hans's phobia of horses Freud highlights how Hans's phobia is formed through a *condensation* of unconscious thoughts relating to his Oedipal conflict, namely his sadistic sexual desire towards his mother and his hostile and rivalrous feelings towards his father. As Butler (1997) points out, Freud's theorizing of the Oedipus complex assumes that heterosexuality has already been accomplished. It presupposes that which it claims to explain. Freud strongly asserts in his reflections on Little Hans's development that homosexuality arises from a fixation at the point of transition between auto-eroticism and "object-love". Freud's theorizing of phobias is therefore rooted in an assumption which is, itself, homophobic. To apply Freud's analysis of phobias in groups two and three to homophobia is untenable.

If the homophobia on which Freud's theorizing is predicated, is normalized, and not regarded as a symptom, can homophobias be usefully considered as belonging to Freud's first category of phobias, exemplified by the fear of snakes? Fears such as this, however, obviously do arise in some cultures (although not all, as Freud claims), and are regarded as socially acceptable or comprehensible within a particular cultural frame or belief system. They are therefore, similarly to homophobia, not treated as "symptoms".

Homophobes and character types

In an interesting move, Young-Bruehl, in her book *Anatomy of Prejudice,* offers an analysis of homophobia in which she specifies three different homophobic character types, namely obsessional, hysterical, and narcissistic. Although these categories are derived from psychoanalytic theory, Young-Bruehl stresses that she does not view people who are prejudiced as any more pathological than any others. Rather, she claims to present descriptions of the different relationships these groups appear to have to homosexuals.

According to Young-Bruehl, the obsessional attitude is character- ized by a view of homosexuality as dirty, degenerate, and feminizing. It is associated with financial power and AIDS. The world therefore needs to be cleansed of gay men. Hysterical characters need homo- sexuals, but "keep them in their place". Homosexuals act out the desires which they prohibit in themselves and they can punish them for it. They can watch gay pornography vicariously but return to their heterosexual world " 'forgetting' that (they) ever left or what (they) did" (Young-Bruehl, 1996, p. 158). A narcissistic relation to homosexuality is revealed in members of same-sex groups which are implicitly, yet strongly defined as non-homosexual, for example, men's teams, clubs, and military units. Young-Bruehl's descriptions are useful as snapshots which succinctly and vividly convey a range of homophobic orientations to the world. She does stress that posi- tions of dominance and alienation for any of these groups are con- stantly shifting and that social and political conditions and purposes "operate as galvanizing ideologies and organizing ideas" (Young- Bruehl, 1996, p. 342). However, as my account of Teresa's struggles with her homophobia towards her son in her analysis highlight, the categories theorized by Young-Bruehl are too sharply delineated and do not sufficiently allow for the shifting complexities of homo- phobic attitudes.

Homosexuality: Whatever next?

In my presentation of Teresa's work in her analysis my focus is on those aspects of Teresa's analysis which concern her explora- tion of conscious and unconscious manifestations of homophobic thoughts and feelings. Many other themes have emerged over the years which have been as or more significant. I feel privileged to be engaged with her exploration of feelings of which she, at times, has felt very ashamed; they are very "at odds" with what she wants to feel towards her son and towards lesbians and gay men in general.

Teresa was already in analysis with me when her son, some years ago, then in his early twenties, "came out" to her as gay. Luigi had decided to "come out" to her because he had begun a relationship with another young man which was important to him. Teresa felt extremely shocked, even if not surprised, and struggled to extend herself to Luigi through her desire for his happiness and against her terror of the possible significances of this for him and for herself. Horrific and threatening images of gay sex and sexualities, and of bizarre lifestyles, cascaded through her, their strangeness threatening to annihilate her. These unspeakable images were also suffused with loss: loss of the picture to which she had clung of her son as a prospective husband and father who would produce grandchildren within a conventional nuclear family situation. Her narrative was interwoven with a number of themes, most of which were conscious: anxieties relating to what were her own, albeit disowned, fantasies of unbounded sexual expression, her terror of the unknown, and feelings of loss in relation to her imagined future. Sometimes her son became the focus, almost arbitrarily, for any of her angry feelings.

Teresa is a highly intelligent woman from an Italian working class, Catholic background who works as a hotel receptionist. She sought analysis because she was suffering from acute anxiety. Teresa's anxiety is constantly shifting its focus and there are times when it is intensely focused particularly on her son's homosexuality. I shall explore here the particular conscious and unconscious associations which have emerged for Teresa in relation to Luigi's sexuality. Through this, I wish to raise the question as to whether this material can augment our understanding of the workings of homophobia in a more general way.

In the early part of her analysis, before her son "came out" to her, Teresa often referred to her fear of God, who was punitive and constantly scrutinizing of her sinfulness. She is also averse to certain images of Christ, recalling a frightened curiosity in her childhood as to what might be underneath his loin-cloth. Teresa does not consciously recall being exposed to explicitly anti-homosexual teachings in the church as a child. However, she does remember her Catholic parents being vehemently anti-gay. Her scrutinizing of her own sexual thoughts and her guilt at these is also very evident.

A strong theme for Teresa is her anxiety that she has "caused" her son's homosexuality. This became focused on her recollection of changing her son's nappy when he was a baby and her disquiet at seeing her son's penis erect; she began to feel that that she must have caused him to have an erection, although she does not recall touching her son inappropriately. Although realizing intellectually that homosexuality is not "caused" in the way she fantasizes, she would return to this anxiety periodically.

This fantasy has generated a number of different meanings, depending on the context. Sometimes it is associated for Teresa with her own childhood experiences of sexually abusive situations. Male sexuality is for her often (although not always) equated with abuse; sexuality between two men therefore appears doubly abusive and disgusts her. Luigi's identification with being gay, placing sex at the foreground of his identity as a man at times seems to embody this notion of abusive masculinity for her. Luigi's moustache emerged in our discussions as unconsciously symbolizing male sexuality, and it becomes the focus of her anxiety and feelings of loss that her small boy is now a sexual man.

A central question is, of course, Teresa's relation to her own sexual desires. She has not had an intimate sexual relationship for over twenty-five years and her son's statement of his sexuality has brought about a crisis of her own. It is unthinkable to Teresa that she may have feelings of attraction towards her son, although she knows that she has never acted upon such a possibility. It is also difficult for her to admit any experiences of same-sex attraction she may have had. In one session when I said to her that her sexuality had been very intertwined with her experience of rejection by her husband she had surprised herself with her tears.

Some weeks later Teresa dreamt that she was enjoying having sex with a person who was half-man and half-woman. This character had male genitals and a very ugly woman's face which was, in the dream, nevertheless erotically attractive to her. I wondered whether the ugly face was an attempt to camouflage the pleasure she was feeling. In a later dream she was making love with her ex-husband. The pleasure was mutual and he was lightly commenting on a physical feature which, actually, is a feature of her own, but which she had attributed to him in the dream. I interpreted to her that perhaps the ex-husband in her dream represented her own sexuality which she was now beginning to claim.

Soon after this, more aspects of her sexuality emerged. She was able to tell me that she had found gay sex on television very erotic until Luigi had come out to her. Teresa also admitted that she felt very uncomfortable about having been attracted to Luigi's partner. She started to feel that her sexuality was "all over the place".

Teresa has found her son's camp aspects very challenging. When he showed her a photo of himself in drag, she had felt very uneasy: what would it lead to? what if he did it in public? it would be different if he were an actor. I reflected on how frightening the unknown was to her. "Or of what I am getting to know: first he says he is gay, then that he has a partner, then that he has a lesbian friend, then that he might give her his sperm ... whatever next?" she replied. I linked this to her childhood memories of always being on the alert and say "perhaps Luigi is "whatever next?". At the end of the session she told me tentatively that, when she is with Luigi, she finds herself making camp gestures. I responded humorously, resonating with the playfulness that I felt she had now begun to allow herself: "you are worried about men being gay, yet here you are as a woman playing at being a camp gay man!"

In a session soon after this Teresa told me that she had dreamt of trying to stop wild animals coming after her. When I reflected on whether these were aspects of herself, her own "wildness", she told me how unbearable it had been to watch a television documentary about a woman scarred by a hysterectomy who had succeeded in becoming a belly-dancer. It felt "too much". I reflected that perhaps the idea of feeling pleasure in, and a connection to, her body and her sexuality felt "too much" for her. Later in the session I suggested that gay men's public identification with their sexualities felt "too much" in a similar way.

It is striking that Teresa's homophobic feelings have been particularly intensified at a time when she has also been struggling with her feelings of being very neglected by her mother (who also had not been able to protect her from her abusive experiences of men). One evening, sitting in her armchair with angry thoughts towards her son, followed by thoughts about whether she had touched him inappropriately, and then a feeling of completely shutting off from him, she said to herself, "so, this is what my mother feels towards me". In a dream, which marked the end of her preoccupation with whether she had abused her son, she "saved the baby" (her words).

Taking hold of a baby which was dangling upside down with wires coming from it, connected to nothing and no-one, she had turned it upright and felt a huge relief.

Teresa's anger towards her son is often a displacement of anger towards other close friends or relatives. We have both wondered if Luigi appears to be a safer target for her feelings because of her assumption that, as her son, he will always be there for her. Furthermore, Luigi's sexuality is culturally sanctioned as a scapegoat and her rage, through its displacement, feels justified.

In her exploration of themes associated with her homophobia or homophobias Teresa's experience of me in the transference shifts between various positions. She relies on me as the mother who, she hopes, can save her from being consumed by her panics and her anger in relation to her son. She has never asked me about my sexuality. This is something Teresa doesn't seem to want to know about and I think that my openness to the ambiguity of sexuality (of which I think she is aware) is crucial to her.

Can any of these reflections from Teresa's sessions contribute to an understanding of the unconscious sources of, or workings of, homophobias? My answer to this is both yes and no. There are significant dangers in making generalizations on the basis of one individual or a small number of individuals' experiences. Quantification is not a solution to complexity. As Noreen O'Connor and Joanna Ryan point out, this tendency on the part of psychoanalysts to theorize lesbian sexuality on the basis of a small number of cases has been extremely limiting. I am neither offering a definitive explanation of homophobia nor claiming that there are inherent acultural features to homophobia, as has been claimed in classical psychoanalytic theorizing with regard to homosexuality. The value of case examples is that, like reading fiction, they can extend *possibilities* of thinking and raising questions about individuals" experiences and alert us to their complexities: they do not and should not claim to offer definitive and universal explanations of certain experiences.

My reflections in this chapter contain a number of dominant themes: the role of religious opinion which is likely to have been absorbed by her parents and herself, the question of her "causing" her son's homosexuality with the implicit assumption that his gay orientation is negative, her own, often abusive, experiences of masculine sexuality, her anxieties in the face of the "unknown", the "whatever next?", her fears of the possible fluidity of her own sexuality, of pleasure in, and enjoyment of it. Enfolded in her phobia or "condensed" within it, to draw on Freud's concept, are Teresa's personal experiences in relation to sexualities but these are not acultural or ahistorical. The experiences she describes are specific to her lived relationships in her class and religious background and her gender.

A neo-Foucauldian analysis allows for interpretations, which do not pre-suppose a split between the psychic and the socio-historical and cultural. It addresses how her narrative and identity have been shaped by a number of discourses: religious (Catholic), psychoanalytic (the notion of her son's homosexuality as being "caused" by his relationship with her), and those relating to gender in which masculinity is characterized as dominant, women's sexuality is deemed threatening (particularly at the time at which Teresa was growing up), and which designate heterosexual desire as natural. Teresa's homophobia might conceptualized as a "condensation" (to use Freud's term) of these discourses. But this is not to assume that this condensation is static or to deny the individuality of her experience. Is such an analysis sufficient for addressing Teresa's experiences in the analytical relationship or for an analysis of the operations of homophobia in more general terms?

Homophobia and melancholia

Through her marriage of Freud's and Foucault's work Judith Butler argues for an integration of the concept (not used by Foucault) of the "psychic" with his analysis of discursive practices and the operations of power. Her project concerns the question of how to theorize the subject's incorporation of social norms without assuming a pre-existent split between internal and external realities. Butler proposes that the foreclosure of homosexual desire is foundational to heterosexuality from the beginning of life. Since the loss of a person of a similar gender whom one has loved cannot be acknowledged, it cannot be mourned: "I have never loved" someone of a similar gender and "I have never lost" any such person" (Butler, 1997, p. 23). As Freud describes, the inability to mourn results in melancholia. Since the foreclosure of homosexual love is "the condition of possibility for social existence" (Butler, 1997, p. 24) heterosexuality is, Butler argues, permeated with melancholy: it is predicated on an unmourned loss. This is not the loss of an attachment that has been made and then disavowed. The form of the attachment has itself been structured through foreclosure, a "mourning for unlived possibilities" (Butler, 1997, p. 139). The girl acquires her gender through the repudiation of her desire for her mother and the positioning of her as a prohibited object in a melancholic identification. The boy's gender identity heterosexually is achieved by his repudiation of the feminine: his desire for the feminine is scarred by this such that he "wants the woman he would never be" (Butler, 1997, p. 137). The more virulently he defends his "masculinity" the more accentuated is his melancholy in relation to the loss of the possibility of homosexual desire. This, she argues, is inevitable where there is no public recognition of the loss which might allow it to be fully grieved. Butler does not assume that melancholia in relation to gender and sexual identifications is limited to heterosexuals; where these are rigidly established for lesbians and gay men there is also the loss of heterosexual possibilities.

Butler presents a developmental account of heterosexual subjectivity but she does not make claims for its universality. Through Foucault, her theorizing challenges any reliance on ahistorical notions of drives and repression, arguing instead that sexualities are "produced". However, diverging from Foucault and reinstalling the notion of the psychic, Butler attempts to explore the meaning for the subject of the prohibition against homosexuality, through Freud's theorizing of melancholia. She emphasizes that the repudiation she describes is not necessary to psychic survival and argues instead for the mobility and fluidity of identifications.

In the light of Butler's work, it is interesting that Teresa's homophobic feelings towards her son have been accentuated at a time when she is experiencing intense feelings of neglect by her mother and fury towards her. Butler's emphasis on the melancholia derived from the inability to mourn the lost object of homosexual love might be relevant here. The homosexuality of her son might, unconsciously, remind Teresa of the homosexual love that was prohibited for her, in her early attachment to her mother. Through her fantasy of sexually touching her son she finds herself in a melancholic identification with her mother as neglectful and abusive enabling Teresa to disavow the loss. She berates herself for her son's homosexuality instead of berating her mother for the unlived possibility of her homosexual attachment to her.

In Foucauldian terms the prohibition against homosexual attachments in Teresa's case is partly constituted by her parents' Catholic discourses of homosexuality as sinful (albeit not made explicit to Teresa). In her account of the subject's subjection to the heterosexual norm Butler does not specify different forms of prohibition, such as those theorized by Foucault. However she does explicitly challenge those notions of "the symbolic" which fail to take into account the multiplicity of ways in which power operates, namely through the reiteration of norms, through demands, and as "formative, productive, malleable, multiple, proliferative, and conflictual" (Butler, 1997, p. 99). It is likely that she is alluding to Lacan here; he claims, for example, that "It is in the *name of the father* that we must recognize the support of the symbolic function which, from the dawn of history, has identified his person with the function of the law" (Lacan, 1966, p. 67).

I think that Teresa is at some level grieving the possibility or acknowledgement of lesbian attachments. She has been in a very strong and intimate, non-sexual relationship with a woman for many years and she has always preferred friendships with women to those with men. However, I think that there is a further feature of her homophobia which is crucial, namely her terror of the "unknown", the chasm opened up for her by differences. This is crystallized in her terrified exclamation, "Whatever next?" at seeing the photograph of her son dressed in drag. This has been a somewhat recurrent, albeit not explicit position, which permeates her narrative. In Butler's terms the "unknown" for Teresa might represent a disavowal of what she wished she could have known, namely homosexual love. However, I think this interpretation does not go far enough.

Homophobia and the Other

Teresa's mother's anxiety and self-absorbed preoccupation with numerous phobias has been a source of terrifying insecurity for her. As a child she was also, always, on the alert for the possible death of her father owing to a chronic illness that he had. Teresa feels that neither parent (although she particularly blames her mother) was ever able to protect her from abusive, or potentially abusive, experiences with men when she was young, or support her when she was terrified. That which is "unknown", unexpected, or ambiguous gives rise to intense anxiety. In her curiosity about what was underneath Christ's loin cloth she both feared and desired knowledge. It was fearful, not only because of her (religious) guilt at being interested in Christ's genitalia, but because whatever she might come to know is never complete and might be even more terrifying. The radical otherness of the Other constantly threatens her.

Levinas is centrally concerned in his theorizing with our relation to the Other. It is for this reason that his work has been of interest to those in culture studies, gender studies, and lesbian and gay studies. His work constitutes a major challenge to the prioritizing of the Same over the Other which permeates Western thought.

According to Levinas, "The Other is what I myself am not. The Other is this, not because of the Other's character, or physiognomy, or psychology, but because of the Other's very alterity" (Levinas, 1947b, p. 83). The "Other" is not another "myself" but is alterity itself. The Other is encountered in the irreducibility of the "face-to-face" relationship. In his account of the face-to-face encounter Levinas emphasizes that the "face speaks. The manifestation of the face is already discourse" (Levinas, 1961, p. 66). This speech is unpredictable and touches us from beyond ourselves. The Other can never be possessed or completely understood; it escapes my power. Furthermore, subjectivity does not pre-exist the relation with others, it is constituted through its openness to the Other. Our awareness of the mortality of the face of the Other demands of us a responsibility to them which does not rely on reciprocity, it is an openness to beyond being. This is an ethical position which does not rely on universal principles; justice for Levinas is rooted in proximity, in responsibility towards one another.

For Levinas what is intrinsic to sexual intimacy is the search for the mysterious. The caress "does not know what it seeks" (Levinas, 1947b, p. 89). He challenges the idea that the relationship with the other is of fusion. Nor is it one of knowing and possessing. Intimacy is a relation to the unknown of the future.

Luigi's homosexuality, for Teresa, symbolizes the Other and it also, as a phobic object, stands in the place of the unknownness of the other. The unconscious references to her fears of the unknown are an important feature of her homophobia. It is not only that she recognizes some of "herself", her prohibited homosexual desire, as an interpretation based on Butler's theorizing might conclude. What is absolutely intolerable to her also is the radical otherness of Luigi, as a man and as gay. Luigi is also now middle-class (Teresa is working-class) but this difference is not as threatening: his achievements in his studies and his work are culturally sanctioned and symbolize her success as a mother. She feels a part of his achievement. His homosexuality, however, symbolizes for her his absolute alterity. Into the absence of what she can know and possess she pours her fantasies. They frighten her, they seem to distance her from him, but they simultaneously bind her son to her. His uniqueness and his alterity, however, resist her power to possess him and to absorb him into the Same and she has murderous thoughts. As Levinas says, "I can only wish to kill an existent which is absolutely independent, which exceeds my powers infinitely, and therefore does not oppose them but paralyses the very power of power" (Levinas, 1961, p. 198).

Conclusion

The theorizing of Foucault, Butler, and Levinas all offer an important contribution to a consideration of what might constitute homophobia or homophobias. As my presentation of Teresa's work in analysis highlights, her conscious and unconscious experiences of homophobia or homophobias are shaped by a number of interweaving discourses through which she has "lived" her sexuality from childhood on. Teresa's associations to Luigi's homosexuality shift in relation to other unconscious concerns which emerge for her at different moments. Enfolded into Teresa's homophobia is also a profound fear of the Other as Levinas conceptualizes it. The forms of Teresa's homophobia are unique to her but my reflections on how they are embedded within her particular socio-historical context might indicate possible directions for interpretations of what is inscribed in the various collective manifestations of homophobia.

CHAPTER TEN

Listening differently in the face-to-face

Noreen O'Connor

Introduction

How does psychoanalysis as praxis stand within discourses of philosophers and psychologists? Currently debates about outcomes of psychotherapeutic, psychoanalytic, and behavioural methods of treating people compete with each other in their claims for the universal objectivity of their own particular research on their practices. Individuals who variously clamour for, or despair of, any other person responding to their psychic suffering may either retreat under the unforgiving weight of demons or they may reach out to whoever is at hand in their socio-cultural context. Debates proliferate on ways to address such individual/social dislocation: maybe the solution is location within religious institutions of, for example, the mosque, the temple, the church, the synagogue, with their concomitant ethically containing mores of family and community. This is a crucial issue because, at the very least, people have survived, loved, and created, within these religions which have existed for thousands of years. But what of the individuals who have lost their place within their beliefs, their society and themselves? When the sense of the past, the present, the future, is obliterated in the fusion of suffocating immobility: where people have no time of their lives or words to speak of it?

Since the development of the human sciences, psychoanalysis, and Jungian analytical psychology in the late nineteenth century there has emerged a myriad of developments of theories with their methodologies, techniques, research, and practices, which claim to help subjective states such as anxiety, insomnia, horror, appetite, depression, and boredom. It is argued that the validity of these techniques has to be seen to be believed; they must be objectively congruent within their own evidential claims and also with the social/political sanctions which classifies their place in society. Serious responsibility is placed on the ethical vigilance of psychotherapeutic validators: Where do they get their codes of ethics? Is it from the practitioners of jurisprudence who formulate laws reflective of the mores of particular societies or states; or judges who interpret them? So, already we have general questions about the status of the kinds of knowledge claimed by practitioners: the kinds of techniques which follow from it, the kinds of ethical judgements which regulate it, and the kind of political society which these ethical values express. All of these questions are formulated in general categories with explicit or implicit assumptions about subjectivity: how we know "who" or what is reality, truth, existence, love, goodness, beauty, justice? Does the question of validity matter if the techniques "work", if they help the person who is in pain? How much or is it possible for us to know the ways in which our own lived presuppositions as analysts, as individuals, affect our technical work? How does our technique relate to the specific individuality of the person who is addressing us in speech/silence?

In the twentieth century existentialist philosophers challenged those philosophers who claimed to elucidate human subjectivity in terms of the objective structures of its consciousness and unconsciousness. Instead they argued that the human, man, was essentially spontaneous. This spontaneity was conceived as ecstatic projection into the world, all consciousness is consciousness of something: the world is not something over and against me but that with which I am engaged, and engages me. Our being-in-the-world is not that of a disembodied mind knowing real things over and against us. We are not monadic beings separate from the world since in our day-to-day lives we are in projects; for example, in making a cup of tea, we do not sit and measure and evaluate the process but rather through doing it we justify it, take responsibility for ourselves for what we do. In doing something we open further possibilities, this engagement is very often described by creative writers when they talk about their fictional characters taking on their own development within the stories which they create; that is, the process of the author's work of writing reveals the characters. This way of conceiving lived subjectivity is counter to thinking of living as a set of instrumental tasks capable of being identified in advance and satisfactorily achieved according to the original goal plan. Existential philosophers have revealed the elusiveness of phenomena we experience in coming to the limits of our representational projects: those phenomena that move us towards intimations of our mortality, our death, our dying.

Many of us wonder about who we are, where we came from in terms of our forebears. In the flux of feelings of our everyday lives; often in times of struggle and suffering, as well as times of being surprised by happiness joy and the sheer delight and excitement of living, we may wonder what it (our existence) is all about. But if our feelings fluctuate, and sometimes feel contradictory of one another how can we speak of a sense of identity of "the self"? Is it a matter of knowing what we feel/think about our lived inherence in life? Is it a question of knowing our identity, in its difference? Heidegger, in *Identity and Difference,* shows that to say, for example, that A is A is more than saying that A possesses all the characteristics of A but that it is the *process* of being A: "The principle of identity speaks of the Being of beings ... To every being as such, there belongs identity, the unity with itself" (Heidegger, 1969, p. 26). What does this mean to us in our day-to-day existence? This sense of unity we struggle to achieve in order to feel happy, how do we know if we achieve it? Are questions about our sense of identity questions about some security we achieve through "self-*knowledge*"?

Levinas sets out on a different path which is to theorize self-identity by exploring it not in terms of a problem of knowledge but as an ethical issue of engaging with how we respond to the otherness of the other person or persons. He discusses this in terms of the relationship of self and Other which occurs in the immediacy of communication: "it is in the risky uncovering of oneself, in sincerity, the breaking up of inwardness, exposure to traumas, vulnerability"

(Levinas, 1974b, p. 48). I shall trace some of Levinas's questions regarding the emergence of the sense of self in lived states of anxieties in the unrelenting weightiness of insomnia, in laziness, and the fatigue of indolence, and I shall highlight how his detailed descriptions of these states as forms of reluctance to exist, "as events" are of particular relevance to psychoanalytic practitioners. Through my discussion of my work with Kieran I will reflect on the relevance of Levinas's phenomenology to my responses to Kieran's crisis in relation to his identities as a white, Irish, heterosexual man and father.

Experiences, events and face-to-face in the consulting room

In his book *Existence and Existents* Levinas wonders about the duality of the relationship between existents (human *beings*) and existence, being. In his preface he mentions that he wrote this while he was in captivity, in a prisoner of war camp. This is not, he says, a claim for profundity or indulgence but an explanation for the absence of any references in his work to important philosophical works published between 1940 and 1945. The context of his being a prisoner of war is very relevant to the themes he pursues; as Lingis, his translator, says: "… this book brings out the processes of unconsciousness, sleep and oblivion which the active and ecstatic subjectivity is backed up against" (Lingis, 1978, p. 9).

Levinas enquires as to whether one can speak of subjectivity without thereby necessarily implying that it exists: can't we just take our existence for granted? While acknowledging that subjects do take up an attitude to their own existence he is exploring not just our struggles with our lived existences but the fissures, the separation that lurks within our familiarity with our existence as a struggle for the future, for endurance and conservation. Crucially Levinas explores the way in which we experience our sense of our existence in our different states and the significance of the fact that inherent in all of our lived engagements, the past, our past, is "there" apart from us and yet it is simultaneously "here" in the now, the instant of my existence. In meditating about "the meaning of life", optimism or pessimism, we are, in a sense, trying to possess our existence reflectively.

By contrast with the traditional Western notion of man over and against the world and "nature", ordering it, Levinas describes what he calls an "event" of birth which occurs in our experiences of phenomena. The "event" is the taking up of a position. Fatigue and weariness are, for example, stances taken up by individuals in relation to existence: they are events of "refusal" (Levinas, 1947a, p. 24), in the sense of being immediately or prereflexively "lived". Levinas stresses the notion of birth as event in order to highlight the vital intertwining of temporal and spatial dimensions in the original singularity of their relationships which produces, constitutes, each of us. Furthermore this singularity is irreducible to a complete reflection in which I could imagine myself as insulated in my isolated controlled knowledge of "myself".

In *Existence and Existents* Levinas begins his analytic description of our situated individuality by focusing on the phenomena of fatigue and indolence. Such phenomena are commonly debated within philosophical thinking in terms of morality or ethics, and conceptualised, for example, as "weakness of will". By contrast with the deliberations of normative ethics Levinas offers us detailed descriptions of embodied experiences of states such as insomnia and lassitude. The ambivalent sense of deadness and yet burden of the dragging weight of one's living body is often described psychoanalytically as depression. Phenomenological and critical analyses of these states highlights the lived ambivalence of inertia and action which are inherent to them.

The crucial challenge of Levinas's work is that of thinking, questioning, differently from any positivistic desire to establish, for example, "truths" or "facts" of depressive states for which we can then formulate "cures". He shows how in their occurrence, insomnia, fatigue, and indolence are "events", positions taken in relation to our existence. One could classify fatigue and indolence as "mental contents" like thoughts, feelings, volitions, "in" the mind, which would be specified as some kind of container. Or one could describe such states in terms of psychopathologies to be cured by isolating the psychic causes and repairing them according to the clinical steps outlined in various theories. Central to the descriptive methodology of phenomenology is the bracketing out of the question of whether or not something exists. As Levinas's work shows, the bracketing out of whether a conscious phenomenon is "real" or "false" enables us to focus on the detail of *how* and *when* phenomena emerge in the psyche. Such phenomena are not "natural objects" which already exist in the brain, then transmitted to "the mind", and are subsequently available for some neutral scientific objective observation. Focus on expressed descriptions allows us to hear, to see, and to respond to the individuality of the other's speaking and its explicit or implicit invocation to us to respond. The question becomes one of who responds to whom rather than one of you, the subject, tell me, the object, *what* I am.

Every human being is born into a world of relationships. These relationships are from the outset constituted by the persons who hear and speak. The baby is therefore born into a world of language. Changes in our relationships occur through our relationships as lived in their different reflective spontaneities as, for example, people change in and through the patient/analyst relationship by engaging in discovering that they can speak/relate differently. Focusing on phenomenological descriptions of experiences of struggle and failure to relate to others and to our environment involves the challenge of entering into the lived sense of being stuck in the weighty weariness of fatigue. It allows the analyst and the patent to articulate and to reflect on the experience of feeling "stuck in treacle", described by many people as a barrier to "living". Levinas criticizes theories of reflection that claim to encompass "the events of our history in a purely formal way, laying them out as contents and covering over their dramatic nature as events" (Levinas, 1947a, p. 24). He argues that when we interpret fatigue and indolence or laziness, as contents of the mind, rather than "events" we fail to realize what is effected, brought about, in them or to see what it is that they are impotently refusing.

Psychoanalytic, and Jungian analytical trainings devote much attention to case material which is interpreted according to the "school" of its teachers. Symptomatology is identified within the material which is derived from and referred back to the basic theoretical model of the psyche that it is operative with its varying distinctions of the normal and the pathological. Reflection on symptomatology is crucial to every analytic practice however theorized because both the analyst and the patient want to find a shared understanding, common language, a new way of talking to each other, in order to guide the therapeutic process.

Classical psychoanalytical theorizing primarily explains these experiences in developmental terms which emerge from elaborations and explorations provided by the analysis of repressed unconscious defence mechanisms, for example, regression, splitting, or displacement. Explanations of impasses in the will to live with hope and enjoyment are traditionally explained by Freud as arising from developmental deviations in relation to unconscious drives which confuse their aims and objects. Klein emphasized the centrality of shifting psychic positions originating in early infancy which an individual lives throughout their temporal existence. Some contemporary psychoanalysts struggle with questions regarding the relation between the mind/body, psychic/social and how such dualities can be challenged in practice.

By contrast, behavioural therapists focus on discovering ways in which the patient consciously thinks and the ways in which this affects their behaviour and resultant feelings in order to facilitate the patient in making conscious changes to their ways of relating to others and to the world. The experienced anxiety of fatigue and indolence would therefore be interpreted as an intentional refusal of a *thought:* for example, the entrenchment of depression would be a refusal to think. This would imply that the event of refusal was reducible to an act following from a clearly thought through assessment of options and consequences, effectively it would be like saying that fatigue and indolence resulted from thinking through the decision not to think.

From Levinas's philosophical position, any account of fatigue and indolence which classifies them as contents of the mind reduces their significance for our lived experiences. It would be to imply that our experiences exist in the flux of consciousness as psychic realities, of being secondary attributes of a foundational substance, namely, the psyche. His notion of "event", the taking up of a position, stresses the complexities of the time, space, individual/social contexts of the production of embodied entities emphasizing the interpretations which are constitutive of any description of a way of existing. For example the phenomenon of "the family" is a much debated entity in political, psychotherapeutic, and personal discourses, it is not a discrete entity whose dynamics can be classified and defined in terms of the linearity of a cause and effect. This contingency is also the case in discussing states of the human psyche and our experiences and descriptions of states such as anxiety, happiness, or depression.

Throughout our book we emphasize the importance of attending to the uniqueness of individuals' experiences. A crucial clinical as well as philosophical question arises: how do theories which claim within their own terms to offer diagnostic and prognostic interpretations/stories as explanations of patients' suffering address individuals' lived perceptions? How can one speak and hear the individuality of the person's experiences? This is a common question, often implicitly operative as despair and secret hope, for people first consulting a psychoanalyst. In telling us their lives the hope is that it might at least interest us and enable a conversational engagement between us which is original. For each of us finding a new way of speaking and listening to another, with others, is finding a new life.

For Levinas, whose reflections on intersubjectivity in *Existence and Existents* are further developed in *Time and the Other*, the "face-to-face" relationship with the Other (the other person whom one encounters) is a "relationship with a Mystery" (Levinas, 1947b, p. 75) and with absolute alterity: "The Other is what I am not. The Other is this, not because of the Other's character, or physiognomy, or psychology, but because of the Other's very alterity" (Levinas, 1947b, p. 83). "The face speaks. The manifestation of the face is already discourse" (Levnias, 1961, p. 66). The "Other" is not another "myself" but is alterity itself. The relationship with the other is not one of "fusion" (Levinas, 1947b, p. 90), although this may be sought. It also does not rely on reciprocity. Levinas's notion of the "face-to-face" is a crucial contribution to a consideration of what occurs in the analytical relationship.

The face-to-face involves a responsibility to the Other, an openness to beyond being, in the sense of an assumption of some shared knowledge of our existence. Rather, responsibility is openness to one's own and the other's vulnerability. As I highlight in my paper "Who Suffers?", "(i)n stressing compassion, the susceptibility of the face-to-face, (Levinas) is saying that in responding to the other whose face "speaks" to me and demands a personal response I am involved in a discourse which is an ethical act"

(O'Connor, 1991, p. 230). According to Levinas, "Moral consciousness is not an experience of moral values, but an access to exterior being—exterior being *par excellence* is the other" (Levinas, 1963, p. 326). An ethical relation is thus one in which one is open and compassionate towards the otherness of the Other, to their uniqueness and to their suffering. Furthermore, as I emphasize in that paper, one can only be an analyst through the "interhuman emergence of one's own suffering" (O'Connor, 1991, p. 233).

Beyond being

Levinas's phenomenological descriptions of the event which produces fatigue and indolence provoke us to begin at the beginning, to slow down and to attend to the experience of recoiling before existence itself. This recoil is in itself the movement that constitutes its existence. This is an invitation to reflect on how such a "depressed" refusal of existence is, in itself, an exploration constitutive of existence.

What happens when our worlds are in pieces, when they are "turned upside-down", when what had seemed to be the rational or logical order, the taken-for-granted sense of our lives is shattered? Levinas specifies this situation as a temporal event, the "instant" or the "moment, and the sense of being within it and without it simultaneously. He describes this moment when the world falls away as one of limit, as a realization of existence, of Being, not as a person or a thing but the sheer fact that one is, what he calls the fact that *there is,* which is neither death nor a pure ego. This relationship with the anonymity of the *there is,* is a relationship which exists yet without being with a specifiable other person or world or thing. This is the sense of existing outside of thought, feeling, or action, outside the familiarity of "economic" life in which "instants are equivalent" (Levinas, 1947a, p. 92) and compensatory.

Phenomena which cannot be explained within, or which are outside of, already established categories of a world conceived of in terms of identity and difference (in which a "thing" is specified by virtue of its being "this" as differentiated from "that") are specified by Levinas as "beyond being". This is a reflection on two fronts: on the one hand we take existence, being, for granted and, on the other, questions can lead us beyond this in order to attend to the issues which are more basic to each of our experiences of lived existence, namely our ethical relationships, our social, personal, responsible relationships with others.

For Levinas the time of the *there is*, is that which, as irreducible to Being, is an occurrence, an event of birth, prior to participation in existence. He approaches this extra-ordinary dimensionality with a complexity of philosophical narrative strategies: "The absence of everything returns as a presence, as the place where the bottom has dropped out of everything, an atmospheric density ... the murmur of silence", neither anyone or anything, "anonymous" (Levinas, 1947b, pp. 46–47).

Insomnia: Relentless vigilance of anonymous existence

Levinas's philosophy offers us ways of reflecting on the paradoxical relationships between our different conceptualizations of notions of consciousness and unconsciousness. His reflections on the relationship of insomnia to existence bring Levinas to the question: "But then what does the advent of a subject consist in?" (Levinas, 1947a, p. 67). Consciousness in its relationship to unconsciousness involves a hesitation in being, in the sense that it can retreat. Consciousness emerges from rest, from sleep, in which we are in contact with the protectiveness of being in a place: "in curling up in a corner to sleep we abandon ourselves to a place ... it becomes our refuge" (Levinas, 1947a, p. 70). Our being is suspended but not destroyed in sleep. Levinas contrasts this "having a place", a way of being, with the kind of consciousness that weighs upon us in insomnia. The subjectivity of the subject begins with its embodiment from this "place" of its own consciousness: this beginning is original in that it "precedes every act of understanding, every horizon and all time" (Levinas, 1947a, p. 71). Levinas explores the metaphors of space and time in order to locate the uniqueness and individuality of human beings. In speaking of the event of human engagement with existence as embodied "position" he emphasizes the irreducibility of each of us to objectification including our attempts to objectify ourselves. Position is "something quite different from all action and labour directed towards the world" (Levinas, 1947a, p. 81). Resting, sleep, takes place in consciousness as position: "But position is the very event of instant as a present" (Levinas, 1947a, p. 72). Our subjectivity is our uniqueness of our "present", time and place.

Levinas's detailed phenomenological analyses of insomnia described in relation to the experience of the relentless weight of anonymous existence are of great relevance to clinical work. He maintains that such descriptive analyses of the phenomenon of insomnia bring him to use terms that lead beyond the notion of a phenomenon capable of being circumscribed by the concept of an ego. In insomnia, Levinas argues, it can seem as if there is no possible break from the restless agitation of living, from the sense of being weighed down by a ceaseless demand to exist. For Levinas, this situation, this "vigilance" (Levinas, 1947a, p. 66), is experienced as an anonymity where there is, or are not, specifiably absent or present "thing" or "things": "One watches on when there is nothing to watch and despite the absence of any reason for remaining watchful. The bare fact of presence is oppressive ... One is detached from any object, any content, yet there is presence" (Levinas, 1947a, p. 65). This vigilance is the opposite of sleep, drowsiness, even the relaxation of absence. Levinas describes this as anonymous nightwatch: "... in insomnia it is the night itself that watches" (Levinas, 1947a, p. 66). It is as though all the thoughts that I have are suspended on nothing. Levinas describes this sense of being the object rather than the subject of "anonymous" thought as the experience of depersonalization and he emphasizes the importance of paying painstaking attention to the experience before interpreting it in terms of the conditions of its emergence.

Levinas argues that this situation cannot be totally encompassed by a descriptive phenomenology because this would presuppose a centralizing ego which could presume to control the anonymity of vigilance. However, phenomenological descriptions are crucial in describing individual experiences which cannot be circumscribed by a general classification. In a sense, Levinas's description of insomnia reminds us that intrinsic to vigilance is an ambiguous relation to the future as an escape from the weight of the present: "The I always has one foot caught in its own existence. Outside in face of everything, it is inside of itself, tied to itself" (Levinas, 1947a, p. 84). It is not simply a matter of tracing intricacies in the past of the psyche in order to draw what is in any sense already "known" to some conscious rational appropriation. In our speaking, we speak to each other and it is through this, Levinas maintains, we can come to a lived acknowledgement of a call to respond to this otherness which is the intrinsic ethical responsiveness in each of us—the "face-to-face" relationship.

Fatigue, weariness and indolence as a beginning

Theories and practices of psychoanalyses and psychotherapy proliferate and compete with claims to solve crises and experiences in peoples lives. I think that all of them, some of them, and none of them, are variously relevant at specific times and circumstances of peoples' lives. In the end the relevance of any them is contingent on the relationship that occurs between the patient and the analyst and on its lived efficacy for the patient. Levinas's work reminds us of the ultimate futility of our efforts to instrumentalise our individuality in a fearful race to find security through illusions of conforming to the ideal of rationality.

What is at issue in depression is weariness, weariness of everything and everyone, and, above all, weariness of oneself. Levinas analyses this situation in terms of weariness of, or fatigue, (he uses these terms interchangeably) in relation to the commitment to existence itself. It is not simply weariness of a particular form of life, of the mundaneity of our surroundings, work, or of the vulgarity or of the cruelty of those with whom we relate. He compares the heaviness of the sense of the irrevocable contract with existence with the forgetting of existence in the "levity of a smile", (Levinas, 1947a, p. 24) where existence floats in its weightlessness and fullness and where its expansion is a vanishing. Weariness is not a judgement about the pain of being; it is the paradox of an existent taking up its existence in the "hesitation" of a refusal (Levinas, 1947a, p. 35). The refusal is *in* weariness: it is not an affective tonality with lassitude as its content. Weariness, as Levinas explores it, is "An evasion without an itinerary and without an end, it is trying not to come ashore somewhere" (Levinas, 1947a, p. 25). Levinas's descriptions highlight subjectivities as always embodied. Although we speak of the body as our possession it is nevertheless constituted through sets of experiences/cognitions. I *am* the materiality of my body in that I am my pain, my breathing. My body is not, according to Levinas, an instrument but is position itself (see Levinas, 1947a, p. 72).

In his reflections on weariness Levinas includes a consideration of indolence. He wonders why indolence is felt as a problem, unsettling us: is it not like the pleasure of spending the morning in bed? He describes how indolence is neither sleep nor somnolence; it renders us prostrate, weighed with idleness and boredom. Like fatigue, indolence also involves a reluctance in relation to action. This does not result from reflection, deliberation on choices. Indolence does not arise from a realization that a certain action is a material impossibility for us or from the consciousness of that impossibility. Levinas argues that, on the contrary, there is an implicit certainty within indolence that a particular action is possible and it is the certainty of this possibility that constitutes what he terms "the bad conscience of indolence" (Levinas, 1947a, p. 25). This aversion to effort is not because we already know, foresee, and dread the kind of pain involved in the effort. In order to appreciate the notion of "indolence" we have to reflect on the specificity of the pain associated with effort. Indolence describes and reveals the beginning of an action, which is also the impossibility of its beginning.

The instant of beginning is more than the imperceptible flow of a span of duration. Beginning is not a kind of freedom: in the instant an action already possesses something, if only the instant itself, and thus can lose it. Levinas describes the movement of an action as both turning to its point of departure and proceeding towards its goal: "The beginning of an act is already a belongingness and a concern for what it belongs to and what belongs to it." (Levinas, 1947a, p. 27). For Levinas, it is the disjunction between the terms "being" and "having", the sense of the ambiguity of our living human attitudes which carry our conscious existence. Action is an inscription in being whereas indolence as a recoil from action is hesitation before existence.

Levinas speaks of the dual aspects of our sense of existing in terms of our being both a self and an ego. He illustrates this duality of our "selves" by reference to the Greek myth of Narcissus who, in attempting to possess himself in his image, finds that he is surprised by its shadow which challenges the "innocence" of his identificatory sense of himself. Similarly, in a Russian folktale Little John, when sent to take lunch to his father working in the fields, decided to get rid of it by tossing it to his own shadow. However, the shadow persisted in clinging to him like "a last and inalienable possession" (Levinas, 1947a, p. 28). Being burdened with oneself is not a calmness of serene wisdom nor an idea which can be distanced from "me" as simply the psychological content of pain. It is "being afraid of life which is nevertheless a life"; this joyless aversion to existence is exemplified in the reflexivity of the verb "to be", one is oneself (on s'est). (Levinas, 1947a, pp. 28–29). Levinas describes fatigue as apprehending and abhorring the burden of existence; indolence is a kind of negation, refusal, an attitude of letting existence get on without oneself. Indolence reveals the tragedy of being in the sense of being profoundly fatigued by the future. This is not a matter of having thoughts about the future and holding back from action. Levinas is connecting being and action by reflection on the realization that there is a sense that underpinning "one has to do" is the "one has to be".

In order to develop the complexity of such "doubling-up" Levinas engages in a further analysis of fatigue. Fatigue, which is often conceived as purely physical in its presentation, experienced as numbness, a curling into oneself, is not, according to Levinas, reducible to muscular exhaustion or toxicity as classified by psychologists and physiologists. As a philosopher he wonders about it by "putting" himself in the instant of fatigue and tries to discover how it comes about. Rather than treating fatigue as a symptom whose meaning can be encompassed by its identification, cause or causes designating the prognosis for its cure Levinas brackets such attempts to fix the truth or reality of fatigue in order to analyze it phenomenologically, that is, to focus on it as a phenomenon emergent in consciousness. This attention reveals the hidden event which the instant effects, brings about which is not reducible to specifying it as an outcome or effect of a cause: "… to scrutinize the instant, to look for the dialectic which takes place in a hitherto unsuspected dimension, is the essential principle of the method which we have adopted." (Levinas, 1947a, p. 30).

Levinas follows this statement by saying that it is by the application of his investigations that clarification of his principle emerges. I think that this reflection is a key to reading and struggling to understand what he has to say. There is, in a sense, a consistency between his meticulous deliberations on hitherto taken for granted phenomena, both a patient invitation and an invitation to patience that is true to both his phenomenological and Talmudic traditions.

Between effort and fatigue

Levinas discusses the relationship between effort and fatigue as the lag between being and that to which it remains attached. Fatigue is not, in his terms, the *cause* of the impossibility of following through an action towards a goal; it is in the slackening itself. To consider effort only in relation to constraint would be to classify it, to confine it to being a matter that is incumbent on our will. The instant of effort compromises our freedom in the immediate way in which its tension is a "lurching" out of fatigue and a falling back into it. As an event, effort is intrinsic to the present which it also lags behind. This is not simply a description of a finite being who is too weak for the world but a call alerting us to the fact that concrete human experiences of effort and fatigue cannot be accounted for solely in terms of action and resistance: "On the contrary, it is by starting with the instant of effort and its internal dialectics that we shall perhaps be able to grasp the notion of activity and its role in human existence" (Levinas, 1947a, p. 32). The duration of effort is made up of stops. In the duration of work effort is not like an impulse bent over an instant to come.

To act is to take on a present, to be irrevocably committed and subject to it: it is in this sense that fatigue is conceived of as the self-contradictory moment of a present which lags behind itself: "The pain of effort or fatigue is wholly made of this being condemned to the present" (Levinas, 1947a, p. 35). I think that this is helpful in thinking about the relentlessness of the present which is felt often when people feel trapped by, for example, what is described as obsessive compulsive behaviour or depression (see my account of Kieran's work in analysis below).

In this "tak(ing) up of the instant through effort" we are committed to "existing in a pure event" which is not a relationship with "any thing" but constitutes an attachment to things in the world for which we have an appetite (Levinas, 1947a, p. 37). The "taking up of an instant" involves intention, argues Levinas. He emphasizes that he is using the term "intention" in its ordinary sense of being animated by desire. He emphasizes that he is speaking of intention as desire, not desire as a care for existence. In (intention as) desire, he argues, I am not concerned with being but only with the object that will satisfy my desire. He argues, for example, that we do not eat in order to live; we eat because we are hungry. He does hold, however, that we *implicitly, unconsciously,* presuppose that desire goes beyond its object, the desirable.

Consciousness and the unconscious

Levinas points out that what is termed the "discovery of the unconscious" is a contradiction in that such a conceptualization interprets the unconscious as equivalent to another consciousness. He regards this as a failure to recognize the ontological function of the unconscious and its relationship with the clarity of consciousness. He calls "consciousness" sincerity, by contrast with the obscurity, and ambiguity, of the unconscious. According to Levinas our being-in-the-world as intention constitutes an affirmation that the peculiar structure of consciousness gives significance to all the "infiltrations" of the unconscious in the world. For Levinas, an unconscious aspect of our psyche is operative anterior to the emergence of the world as we experience it.

Levinas does not consider that the unconscious is constituted through its opposition to the consciousness, as an obscure world running parallel but similarly significant to the "daylight" world. He argues that there is a proximity between unconsciousness and consciousness, but they are not fused into one. Levinas describes the relationship between these different but interrelated states in terms of "mental reservations" which cannot be converted into conscious intentions. They "murmur in the very activity of thought, as in a wink, made up of looking and not looking" (Levinas, 1947a, p. 68) in the same moment. Here Levinas is reflecting on his basic preoccupation which runs through all of his work, namely, that we cannot reduce our self-knowledge to some sort of determinative self-knowledge which gathers the lived temporal dispersion of our engagements to a kind of universal present in which the "truth" of ourselves is fully understood. For example, many psychoanalytic and psychotherapeutic theories and models of the human psyche and its vicissitudes might interpret insomnia in terms of varieties of anxiety neuroses caused by repressed or denied developmental legacies. It is assumed that change occurs through an *explanation* of their unconscious dynamisms.

Kieran's fatigue

The following account of my work with Kieran illustrates how Levinas's theorizing of insomnia, fatigue, indolence, and effort guided me in the positions I took up in our particular analytical relationship. My verbal responses to Kieran are not necessarily expressed in Levinas's terms as it is the specific language of Kieran's own descriptions which concern me. However my orientation and attention to how his depression pervaded his embodiment in the light of Levinas's work was crucial.

Kieran began his therapy by saying that he was "in the prime of his life", as his friends and family had been reminding him, the problem was it didn't mean anything to him. His sister-in-law, a good friend, had suggested maybe he should just talk it out with someone before considering taking antidepressants which had also been suggested to him. "So here I am". He asked me if there was much point in his coming to therapy since he didn't think that talking changed anything and even if it did he didn't have much to say for himself. I was moved by his sense of being defeated by life but also by his reluctant hope that something could change. I suggested that we could begin to meet regularly and he could see how it felt.

In Kieran's terms he "had it all", educated at one of the best boys' private school in Ireland, a first degree in computer science, married to the woman with whom he had fallen in love, three "gorgeous" children. The problem was that the world was grey, there was nothing to live for; looking at his wife's pleading eyes and the children snuggling up to him, all he was aware of was a kind of deadness, a sense that there was something missing that he couldn't feel. As I listened, I felt that he was talking for the sake of talking, doing what was expected of him and that if I said this he would have been very hurt. I was reminded of Levinas's descriptions of weariness and fatigue and silently wondered if Kieran's depression was implicitly a refusal to meet others' expectations. In his speaking I realized that I had to slow down my associations to his manifest speech and attend to the details of his daily life. In a sense I felt that this was similar to listening and responding to a small child but it was also a discovery (for both of us) of his feelings in his lived presents.

Kieran and Marie had lived together first then got married in Dublin. She is an art teacher and he worked for a company a friend had set up. He wanted more of a challenge before having the kids so off they came to London. First few years was "all go", challenges but something changed, first not wanting to get up, not feeling close to Marie after sex, annoyed by the children, bored by his job, feeling driven by a boss who was "hyper in every way". He could hardly find words for the guilt and shame that he felt about his loss of libido and asked me whether I thought he wasn't a regular man. I explored with him his forgottenness of sexual desire, his adolescent excitement about his sexuality but the fearful threat that it represented: as well as being a sinner he could get a girl pregnant and ruin her life and his own and his family's lives. Exhaustion exuded from his arm as he tried to gesture the deadness away. He sort of remembered what it was like to feel so he would look at his wife and children but he was "in the glass box". "They keep asking me why can't I just get on with it, after all I have everything going for me". Kieran's gestures expressed the ambiguity that Levinas ascribes to indolence, namely that it describes and reveals the beginning of an action which is also the impossibility of its beginning.

"Do you feel that no one wants to hear what you are trying to say about hard it is?" I asked him. "Yes, because she tries and then gets cross because it doesn't make any difference. When I'm wake in the night, I watch Marie sleeping, then I go into the children's rooms; there they are, years wishing they would sleep, now it doesn't matter, I try playing patience, just waiting for the morning light". "I do make the effort to come here; Marie and the family think I should come three times a week" he looks at me his face drawn but with a kind of hesitant, reluctant, turn in his waking sleep: politely, "I hope that's alright with you?" I heard in the question the language that carried him despite himself, his felt sense of himself as hopelessly forlorn as he slowly unfurled himself to stand up. As in Levinas's descriptions of insomnia intrinsic to Kieran's sleeplessness there was an almost impalpable infiltration of the future. His commitment to the therapy also indicated this.

Kieran said he was sick of himself, of wondering about what it was that he was looking for. Mostly he said that he wanted time to think about it all, whatever "it" was: "You'd know that from philosophy wouldn't you?" I said that I did understand his bewilderment about the stuck way that he felt but that I did also think that it was important that he could value his "time to think" and that he did realize that I also valued his doing that for himself. Kieran spoke, as time went on, of his parental family: particularly his growing interest in the past and its influence on the identities of his father and grandfather. The past for him was, he said, Irish history and it mattered because it was his: he speculated on his grandfather's allegiances in Dublin after the civil war in the 1920s, he wondered whether I thought that the success of his family's business grew partly from enduring unquestioned political allegiances and their rewards. He often began such reflections by smiling shyly at me.

In one session Kieran found himself ironically intoning a line of a republican song: "And the Angelus Bell o'er the Liffey swell, rang out through the foggy dew". To Kieran's astonishment sentences, words, and phrases, came tumbling out at speaking of his great grandparents and their treatment by the landlords of Mayo and the misery of the famine. His grandparents, meeting in a Dublin tenement, "the harshness of it, how did they survive? ... They knew what it was like to fight to survive, for the family, the food, clothes and a roof over their heads, why wasn't any of this real to me growing up, even in the Leaving Cert. (similar to British "A" level) history class? I never felt any of it was to do with me". Through his speech Kieran was taking up a new position in relation to the past, not as a conscious decision, but through speaking in our "face-to-face" relationship.

Usually Kieran moved between staccato statements and animated elaborations of the uselessness of talking, sometimes reluctantly acknowledging that, since I was Irish, I might have some clues as to what he was trying to get at. In listening I was aware of the seductive allure of chatting about our common cultural heritage but also of the significance of this for our relationship in terms of the complexities of transferences, positive and negative. I realized that I had to be vigilant about being bewitched by an apparent "common language". He noticed my animated interest in the school he had been to; I had too had realized this when I found myself wondering how their rugby team was getting on. This talk of his school reminded me of a boyfriend of my youth who had captained it. As with most of our psychoanalytic relationships there were two of us with all of our unconscious engagements variously constellated in the intricacies of our conscious speaking and being together. One obvious interpretation of this instance of my response is that I wanted to move him to life, action and desire and that I wanted to escape being with the hopelessness he was expressing. I also wondered with him if my interest in his school echoed the exhortations of his father to "get stuck in, be one of the lads".

These kinds of associations are central to our work and their crucial clinical relevance lies in our openness to the way in which as analysts, we wonder, how we wonder about the similarities, differences, indifferences, between each of us and the uniqueness and originality of each of our patients. Each patient can simultaneously at different times exemplify a range of conflicting symptoms which are familiar and commonly elaborated and debated in psychoanalytic literature. Basic to all of the common struggles of patient and analyst to make some sense of the patient's impasse and to tolerate and explore ambiguity is the belief that it is the relationship between us that matters in the sense that it is the material from which the patient can move. Interpretation, specification, delineation, and creation of relationships is the work of psychoanalysis.

Kieran's lethargic reluctance to "bother at all" was connected to what he called his "ponderances" on the stories of his grandparents and parents: "What is the point? There is nothing to say, it's all over, they've done it, nothing now for me: I know there's Marie and the kids but ... I dunno". "We can't go back, there is nothing in Dublin, the same old crowd saying the same cheery stuff, I'm not a part of it, I played the game, in the end do I want my kids to do it, to pretend?" Kieran was sensitive to the seriousness with which I wondered about his traumatic realization that he could not live a life mapped out as he had imagined it. I was reminded of Levinas's description of fatigue as a hand "that is holding on to what it is letting slip, even when it has let drop but remains taut with the effort" (Levinas, 1947a, p. 30). Because of my speaking of his experience as mattering to me, of my naming his sense of failure as a "breakdown" because of something in his psychic past dragging him down, smothering his sense of his future, he said he knew what I meant, it was true that the notion of living the life a successful son of a Dublin businessman plunged him into frightening feelings of paralysis. He said that it began to be clear to him that he had been feeling haunted by a feeling that unless he had an identity which was in some way transparent and validated by his father he could not exist as a man. His family in Ireland heard that he was in analysis and half-joked their concern that he might end up joining the "moonies"; this now made him feel angry because he said that, as painful as it was, making a relationship with me was what was helping him to see his living more clearly for himself and not through anyone else's eyes. I was very moved at his courage in saying it and at the trust in both of us that it expressed.

Depression such as Kieran's is sometimes described as a crisis of identity—as a man, a son, grandson, father, husband, a successful and respected professional. There is a common tension for any analyst between his/her claims to hear the voice, the individuality of the patient's speaking of themselves and the generality and "objectivity" of the clinical interpretative framework which classifies and categorises such speaking. We know that notwithstanding our reflections on our own value systems, prejudices, and limitations that we are engaged in relationships with our patients. Kieran's crisis, in the form of fatigue or depression revolved around his refusal of both the identity which was expected of him and his terror and refusal of his own individuality. This is not at all to assume that there is an individuality that one can possess like a thing or an object or in isolation.

Levinas challenges the notion of the human subject as characterized by freedom and reason who can, in a sense, dominate the world. His major concern is to illustrate the "interiority" through which man as subject, as an "I" begins to emerge. For Levinas the world is what we inhabit, all that we do is living, whether in our eating, working, walking, arguing, reading, loving, hating, laughing or crying. To be in the world is to feel freed from a preoccupied concern with self-understanding based on a conception of existence as the movement of instincts. Levinas is exploring subjectivity through dimensions whose configuration emerges in order to draw us beyond the familiarity of understanding. This is not a matter of tracing past intricacies which are already drawn in order to bring what is already "known" to conscious rational appropriation but is rather, as I show in my work with Kieran, a lived acknowledgment of a call to respond to this otherness which is intrinsic to each of our own selves—the face-to-face relationship:

> The unravelling of the plot of saying does not belong to a language qua said, does not belong to the last word. Saying signifies without stopping in the said, does not part from (come from) an ego, does not go back to a disclosure in a consciousness (Levinas, 1974b, p. 190, Note 34).

REFERENCES

Ahmed, S. (2006). *Queer Phenomenology.* Durham and London: Duke University Press.

Bartlett, A., King, M. & Smith, G. (2009). The response of mental health professionals to clients seeking help to change or redirect same-sex sexual orientation. *BMC Psychiatry* 9:11.

Benjamin, J. (1990). Recognition and destruction: an outline of intersubjectivity. In S. Mitchell and L. Aron (Eds.), *Relational Psychoanalysis, the Emergence of a Tradition.* Hillsdale, NJ: The Analytic Press, 1999.

Bernauer, J.W. & Mahon, M. (1994). The ethics of Michel Foucault. In: G. Gutting (Ed.), *The Cambridge Companion to Foucault.* Cambridge: Cambridge University Press.

Bion, W. (1970). *Attention and Interpretation.* London: Karnac, 1993.

Binswanger, L. (1946). The case of Ellen West, trans. W. Mendel and J. Lyons. In: R. May, E. Angel, H. Ellenberger (Eds.), *Existence.* New York: Basic Books, 1958, pp. 237–364.

Binswanger, L. (1946). The existential analysis school of thought, trans. E. Angel. In: R. May, Ellenberger (Eds.), *Existence.* New York: Basic Books, 1958, pp. 191–213.

Boss, M. (1979). *Existential Foundations of Medicine and Psychology,* trans. S. Conway and A. Cleaves. Northvale, NJ and London: Jason Aronson, 1994.

175

Butler, J. (1993). *Bodies That Matter*, NY and London: Routledge.

Butler, J. (1997). *The Psychic Life of Power.* Stanford: Stanford University Press.

Chanter, T. (2008). *The Picture of Abjection: Film, Fetish and the Nature of Difference.* Bloomington and Indianapolis: Indiana University Press.

Chodorow, N. (1978). *The Reproduction of Mothering,* Berkeley, Los Angeles and London: University of California Press.

Cooper, E. (1986). *The Sexual Perspective, Homosexuality and Art in the Last 100 Years in the West,* Routledge and Kegan Paul: London and New York, 1994.

Cottingham, J. (1995) in T. Honderich (ed.) *The Oxford Companion to Philosophy,* London and New York: Oxford University Press.

De Beauvoir, S. (1949). *The Second Sex.* Harmondsworth: Penguin, 1974.

Descartes, R. (1968) *Discourse on Method and The Meditations,* trans. F.E. Sutcliffe, Harmondsworth, UK: Penguin Books.

Dosse, F. (2006). Travail et devoir de mémoire chez Paul Ricoeur. In F. Dosse, A. Finkelkraut, J-C. Guillebaud (Eds.), *La Mémoire, Pour Quoi Faire?* Paris: Les Editions de l'Atelier/Les Editions Ouvrières, pp. 75–103.

Ellenberger, H.F. (1970). *The Discovery of the Unconscious.* New York: Basic Books.

Ellis, M.L. (1994). Lesbians, gay men and psychoanalytic training. *Free Associations* Vol. 4 (4): 501–517. [Translated for this edition] at the end of the reference

Ellis, M.L. (1999). *Sexuality and Historicity in Merleau-Ponty's Phenomenology of Perception,* M.A. Thesis (unpublished), Middlesex University.

Ellis, M.L. (2008). *Time in Practice: Analytical Perspectives On the Times of Our Lives.* London: Karnac.

Fanon, F. (1952). *Black Skin, White Masks,* transl. Charles Lamm Markmann, London and Sydney: Pluto Press, 1986.

Ferguson, A., Zita, J.N. & Addelson, K.P. (1982). On compulsory heterosexuality and lesbian existence: defining the issues. In N. Keohane, M.Z. Rosaldo and B.C. Gelpi (Eds.), *Feminist Theory, A Critique of Ideology.* Brighton: Harvester Press.

Flax, J. (1993). *Disputed Subjects, Essays on Psychoanalysis, Politics and Philosophy.* New York: Routledge.

Foucault, M. (1969). *The Archeology of Knowledge,* trans. A. Sheridan Smith. New York: Pantheon, 1972 and London: Routledge, 1995.

Foucault, M. (1978). *The History of Sexuality, Volume One, An Introduction,* trans. R. Hurley. Harmondsworth: Penguin.

Foucault, M. (1984). Nieztsche, genealogy, history, trans. D.F. Bouchard and S. Simon. In: D. Bouchard (Eds.) *Language, Counter-Memory, Practice,* Ithaca, New York: Cornell University Press.

Foucault, M. (1987). Questions of method: an interview with Michel Foucault. In: K. Baynes, J. Bohman, and T. McCarthy (Ed.), *After Philosophy, End or Transformation?* Cambridge: MIT Press.

Freud, S. (1900a). *The Interpretation of Dreams. Standard Edition Vol.* 4–5. London: Hogarth Press.

Freud, S. (1905d). *On the Theory of Sexuality. Standard Edition Vol.* 7. London: Hogarth Press.

Freud, S. (1909b). Analysis of a Phobia in a Five Year Old Boy. *Standard Edition Vol.* 10:3. London: Hogarth Press.

Freud, S. (1912e). Recommendations to Physicians Practising Psycho-Analysis. *Standard Edition Vol.* 12. London: Hogarth Press.

Freud, S. (1914g). Remembering, Repeating and Working-Through, *Standard Edition Vol.* 12. London: Hogarth Press.

Freud, S. (1917[1916–1917]). Anxiety. In *New Introductory Lectures on Psychoanalysis*, Part Three. *Standard Edition Vol.* 16. London: Hogarth Press.

Freud, S. (1920a). Psychogenesis of a Case of Female Homosexuality, *Standard Edition Vol.* 18. London: Hogarth Press.

Freud, S. (1920g). Beyond the Pleasure Principle. *Standard Edition Vol.* 18. London: Hogarth Press.

Freud, S. (1923b). The Ego and the Id. *Standard Edition Vol.* 19. London: Hogarth Press.

Freud, S. (1926d). Inhibitions, Symptoms and Anxiety. *Standard Edition Vol.* 20. London: Hogarth Press.

Freud, S. (1927e) Fetishism. *Standard Edition Vol.* 21. London: Hogarth Press.

Freud, S. (1937d). Constructions in analysis. *Standard Edition Vol.* 23. London: Hogarth Press.

Fromm, E. (1978). *The Crisis of Psychoanalysis.* Harmondsworth, UK: Penguin Books.

Gadamer, H.G. (1975). *Truth and Method,* trans. J. Weinsheimer and D.G. Marshall. London: Sheed Ward, 1975.

Green, A. (2002). *Time in Psychoanalysis,* trans. A. Weller. London: Free Association Books.

Grosz, E. (1994). Refiguring lesbian desire. In: L. Doan (Ed.), *The Lesbian Postmodern*, New York and Chichester: Columbia University Press, pp. 67–84.

Grosz, E. (1995). Bodies and knowledges; feminism and the crisis of reason. In: L. Alcoff and E. Potter (Ed.), *Feminist Epistemologies.* New York: Routledge, pp. 187–215.

Hammonds, E. (1994). Black (w)holes and the geometry of black female sexuality, *Differences* 6, 2 and 3: 25–144.

Heidegger, M. (1962). *Being and Time,* trans. J. Macquarrie and E. Robinson. Oxford, UK: Basil Blackwell, 1990.

Heidegger, M. (1969). *Identity and Difference.* New York: Harper and Row.

Heidegger, M. (1947). *Platons Lehre von der Wahrheit: Mit einem Brief Uber den "Humanismus",* Berne, Franke, 1954.

Hoffman, E. (1989). *Lost In Translation.* London: Vintage.

Hogan, L. (Ed.) (1997). *Feminist Approaches to Art Therapy.* London and New York: Routledge and Kegan Paul.

Hogan, L. (Ed.) (2003). *Gender Issues in Art Therapy.* London: Jessica Kingsley.

Irigaray, L. (1985). *This Sex Which Is Not One,* trans, Catherine Porter, Ithaca, New York: Cornell University Press.

Khan, M. (1964). *Alienation in Perversions.* London: Karnac, 1989.

Klein, M. (1928). Early stages of the Oedipus conflict. In: *Contributions to Psychoanalysis 1921–1945.* London: Hogarth Press, 1948.

Klein, M. (1930). The importance of symbol formation. In: *Contributions to Psychoanalysis 1921–1945.* London: Hogarth Press, 1948.

Klein, M. (1950). On the criteria for the termination of a psychoanalysis. In: *Envy and Gratitude and Other Works 1946–1963.* London: Hogarth Press, 1984.

Klein, M. (1952). Some theoretical conclusions regarding the emotional life of the infant. In: *Envy and Gratitude and Other Works 1946–1963.* London: Hogarth Press, 1984.

Klein, M. (1955). The psychoanalystic play technique: its history and significance. In: *Envy and Gratitude and Other Works 1946–1963.* London: Hogarth Press, 1984.

Klein, M. (1957). Envy and gratitude. In: *Envy and Gratitude and Other Works 1946–1963.* London: Hogarth Press, 1984.

Kearney, R. (1988). *The Wake of Imagination.* London: Routledge, 1994.

Kristeva, J. (1980). *Desire in Language: A Semiotic Approach to Literature and Art,* trans. T. Gora, A. Jardine, and L. Rodiez. Oxford: Blackwell.

Kristeva, J. (1982). *Powers of Horror. An Essay on Abjection,* trans. L. Rodiez, New York: Columbia University Press.

Kristeva, J. (1982b). Psychoanalysis and the polis. In: T. Moi (Ed.), *The Kristeva Reader.* Oxford: Blackwell, 1986, pp. 310–320.

Kristeva, J. (1983). Freud and love: treatment and its discontents. In: T. Moi (Ed.), *The Kristeva Reader.* Oxford: Blackwell, 1986, pp. 238–271.

Kristeva, J. (1984). *Revolution in Poetic Language,* trans. M. Waller, New York: Columbia University Press.

Lacan, J. (1966). *Ecrits,* trans. A. Sheridan. London: Tavistock Publications, 1984.

Laing, R.D. (1961). *Self and Others*. Harmondsworth: Penguin, 1976.

Lear, J. (1998). *Open Minded*. Cambridge, Mass. and London, England: Harvard University Press.

Levinas, E. (1947a). *Existence and Existents*, trans. A. Lingis. The Hague: Martinus Nijhoff, 1978.

Levinas, E. (1947b). *Time and the Other*, trans. R. Cohen. Pittsburgh: Duquesne University Press, 1987.

Levinas, E. (1961). *Totality and Infinity*, trans. A. Lingis. Pitsburgh: Duquesne University Press, 1969.

Levinas, E. (1963). *Difficile Liberté: Essais sur le Judaisme*. Paris: Albin Michel.

Levinas, E. (1967). *En Découvrant l'Existence avec Husserl et Heidegger*. Paris: Vrin.

Levinas, E. (1974a). Collected Philosophical Papers, trans. A. Lingis. The Hague: Martinus Nijhof, 1987.

Levinas, E. (1974b). *Otherwise Than Being or Beyond Essence*, trans. A. Lingis. Duquesne University Press, 1998.

Levinas, E. (1988). Useless suffering, trans. R. Cohen. In: R. Bernasconi & D. Wood (Eds.), *The Provocation of Levinas*, London: Routledge and Kegan Paul.

Levinas, E. (1990). *The Nine Talmudic Readings*, trans. A. Aronowicz. Bloomington: Indiana University Press.

Limentani, A. (1989). Clinical types of homosexuality. In *Between Freud and Klein: The Psychoanalytic Quest for Knowledge and Truth*. London: Free Association Books.

Lorde, A. (1982). *Zami*. London: Sheba Feminist Publishers.

Malinowski, B. in E. Jones, review of Malinowski, B. *Sex and Repression in Savage Society*, *International Journal of Psycho-Analysis* 9, July 1928.

Mann, T. (1924). *The Magic Mountain*. London: Vintage, 1999.

Meltzer, D. (1967). *The Psychoanalytic Process*. Perthshire: Clunie Press.

Meltzer, D. (1979). *Sexual States of Mind*. Perthshire: Clunie Press.

Merleau-Ponty, M. (1962). *The Phenomenology of Perception*, trans. C. Smith. London and Henley: Routledge & Kegan Paul, 1986.

Merleau-Ponty, M. (1964a). The child's relations with others. In: J. Wild (Ed.), *The Primacy of Perception*. Chicago: Northwestern University Press, pp. 96–155.

Merleau-Ponty, M. (1964b). *Signs*, trans. R. McCleary. Evanston, Illinois: Northwestern University Press.

Merleau-Ponty, M. (1970). Phenomenology and psychoanalysis: preface to Hesnard's *L'Oeuvre de Freud*, trans. Alden L. Fisher. In: K. Hoeller (Ed.), *Merleau-Ponty and Psychology*, New Jersey: Humanities Press, 1994.

Mitchell, J. (Ed.) (1986). *The Selected Melanie Klein.* Harmondsworth, Middlesex: Penguin.

Needleman, J. (1967). On a critical introduction to Ludwig Binswanger's existential analysis. In: J. Needleman (Ed. and trans.), *Being-In-the-World, Selected Papers of Ludwig Binswanger.* New York and Evanston: Harper and Row.

Nuñez, R. & Sweester, R. (2006). *Cognitive Science.*

O'Connor, N. (1988). The personal is political: discursive practice of the face-to-face. In: R. Bernasconi and D. Wood (Eds.), *The Provocation of Levinas, Rethinking the Other.* London and New York: Routledge.

O'Connor, N. (1991). Who suffers? In: R. Bernasconi and S. Critchley (Eds.), *Re-reading Levinas.* Bloomington and Indianapolis: Indiana University Press.

O'Connor, N. & Ryan, J. (1993). *Wild Desires and Mistaken Identities, Lesbianism and Psychoanalysis.* London: Virago and New York. Columbia University Press, 1994. London: Karnac, 2003.

Osborne, P. (1995). *The Politics of Time.* London and New York: Verso.

Pontalis, J.B. (1994). The problem of the unconscious in Merleau-Ponty's thought, transl. W. Ver Ecke and M. Greer. In: K. Hoeller (Ed), *Merleau-Ponty and Psychology,* Humanities Press: New Jersey.

Rée, J. (1998). *Heidegger, History and Truth in Being and Time.* London: Phoenix.

Rickman, H. (1964). *Preface to Philosophy.* London: Routledge and Kegan Paul.

Ricoeur, P. (2004). *Memory, History, Forgetting,* trans. K. Blamey and D. Pellauer. Chicago and London: University of Chicago Press.

Roustang, F. (1976). Towards a theory of psychosis, trans. N. Lakacher. In: *Dire Mastery.* Baltimore: John Hopkins University Press, 1982.

Roustang, F. (1983). *Psychoanalysis Never Lets Go,* trans. N. Lukacher. Baltimore and London: John Hopkins University Press.

Ryan, T. (2000). The search for "self" and "other" in therapeutic communities. In: B. Seu (Ed.), *Who am I? The Ego and the Self in Psychoanalysis.* London: Rebus Press, pp. 143–155.

Sabbadini, A. (1989). Boundaries of timelessness. Some thoughts about the temporal dimension of the psychoanalytic space. *International Journal of Psychoanalysis, 70:* 305–313.

Samuels, A. (1993). *The Political Psyche.* London: Routledge.

Sawicki, J. (1994). Foucault, feminism, and questions of identity. In: G. Gutting (Ed.), *The Cambridge Companion to Foucault.* Cambridge: Cambridge University Press, pp. 286–313.

Schaverien, J. (1995). *Desire and the Female Therapist.* London and New York: Routledge and Kegan Paul.

Schaverien, J. (1999). The scapegoat: Jewish experience and art psychotherapy groups. In: J. Campbell, M. Liebmann, F. Brooks, J. Jones, C. Ward (Eds.), *Art Therapy, Race and Culture*. London: Jessica Kingsley.

Segal, H. (1981). Notes on symbol formation. In: *The Work of Hannah Segal, a Kleinian Approach to Clinical Practice, Delusion and Artistic Creativity and Other Psychoanalytic Essays*. London: Free Associations Books, 1986.

Segal, H. (1990). Jacqueline Rose interview. In *Women: A Cultural Review*. London: Oxford University Press.

Skaife, S. (2001). Making visible: art therapy and intersubjectivity. *Inscape*, Vol. 6, No. 2. London: British Association of Art Therapists.

Spillers, H. (1997). All the things you could be by now if Sigmund Freud's wife was your mother. In: E. Abel, B. Christian, H. Moslen (Eds.), *Female Subjects in Black and White*. California: University of California Press.

Socarides, C. (1994). Article in Washington Times, 5 July USA.

Spivak, G. (1990). *The Post-Colonial Critic*. London: Routledge.

Twomey, D. (2003). British psychoanalytic attitudes towards homosexuality. In V. Lingiardi, and J. Drescher (Eds.). *The Mental Health Professions and Homosexuality: International Perspectives*. New York: The Haworth Press.

von Kraft-Ebbing, R. (1886). *Psychopathia Sexualis*. New York: G.P. Putnam's & Sons, 1965.

Walton, J. (1997). Re-placing race in (white) psychoanalytic discourse. In: E. Abel, B. Christian, H. Moslen (Eds.), *Female Subjects in Black and White*, California: University of California Press.

Weeks, J. (1979). *Coming Out*. London: Quartet Books.

Whisman, V. (1993). Identity crises: Who is a lesbian anyway? In: A. Stein (Ed.), *Sisters, Sexperts, Queers*. New York: Plume, New American Library (Penguin).

Whitebook, J. (1995). *Perversion and Utopia*. Massachussetts: MIT.

Wittgenstein, L. (1978). *Lectures and Conversations, Aesthetics, Psychology and Religious Belief*, ed. C. Barrett. Oxford: Blackwell.

Young-Bruehl, E. (1996). *Anatomy of Prejudices*. Cambridge; MA: Harvard University Press.

INDEX

Agoraphobia 140
Alienating interpretations 126
Alienation in Perversions 126
Analysand's non-object-
orientated layers 53
Art therapy
language and
embodiment 121–136
questions of
sexuality in 122–124
Association of
Psychoanalytic
Psychotherapy 16

Being beyond 161
Being-ahead-of-oneself 98
Being-towards-death 98
Binswanger 100
case-example 101
Bisexuality 71
of infancy 72
Bisexual sexualities 121, 123

Blue ribbon tale of 86
Borderline psychosis 52–54
British National Health
Service body 16
British Object Relations
psychoanalyst 53
Butch-femme
identifications 15
Butler, Judith 4

Calendar time 96–97
Cartesian
dualisms 67–70, 77
dualistic thinking 69
tradition 61
Catholicism 20, 29
Christian organization 26, 28
Civil Partnership Act 2004 33
Confrontational hostility 54
Conscious/unconscious 131–137
Consciousness 162, 168
Constitutional monarch 67

Cosmological time 96–97
Creativity and symbolisation 39

Darwinism 14
Defence mechanisms 159
Desexualised ego-libido 69
Desire and the Female Therapist 123
(Dis)continuous identities 95
Domination
    relations of 110
    resistance to 110

Ego
    economic 73–74
    ethnocentric 74–77
    Freud's account
        of gendering 70
    Freud's conceptions
        of familial organization 73
    Freud's
        conceptualisation
        of 67–68, 74
    Freud's formation 39, 60
    gendered 70–73
    identifications 83
    masculinity or femininity 70
    maturity 83
    mediation of 68
    Merleau-Ponty theorises
        subjectivity 61
    reasonable ego,
        mechanics of 61–64
Ego shifting, towards
    body subject 59
Ego-libido, desexualised 69
Ellis, Mary Lynne 11, 59, 95,
    121, 139
English Romantic associations 113
Events in consulting room 156–161
Experiences in consulting
    room 156–161

Face-to face relationship 47, 115
    in consulting room 156–161
    Levinas concept 55
    listening differently in 153–173
    with differences 54–56
Fanon
    psychoanalytic theory 135
    theorizing of women's
        sexuality 135
Father-identification 71
Fatigue 164–167
Femininity 2, 61, 70–71, 73
    Freud's conceptions of 74
Fetishism 85, 89
Foucauldian
    analysis 25
    reduction 101
Foucault, Michel
    history of sexuality 3–4
    theorizing of sexual
        identities 136
Fragility and desperation 22
Freudian phallocentrism
    and ethnocentrism 43
Freud's
    enlightenment
        conceptualization
        of ego 80
    evenly-suspended
        attention, notion of 113–114
    formulation of ego 60
    homophobia reading 140–141
    objectivity 61
    perversion 89–91
    *Psychogenesis of a Case
        of Female
        Homosexuality* 83
    theorising the ego 59, 85
    theory of fetishism 85, 93
    unconscious drives 69
Freud's analysis of dreams,
    Wittgenstein's critique 45

Gadamer's argument,
  Truth and Method 48
Genealogy 107
General Theory of Relativity 97
Geworfenheit 100
Gordon, Stephen 15
Grosz, Elizabeth 6

Hall, Radcliffe, *The Well
  of Loneliness* 15
Heidegger
  analysis of death 99
  future-time 97–100
  Identity and Difference 155
  Letter on Humanism 54
  theorizing of mineness
    of death 115
Heterosexuality 3–4, 7, 9, 16,
  33, 56, 71, 135
  aetiology of 17
  identity 25
The History of Sexuality 13
Hoffman, *Lost In Translation* 106
Homophobes and
  character types 141–142
Homophobia 147–151
  patient 139–151
Homosexuality 3–5, 7, 39, 135, 142,
  144, 148
  cause of 11
  medical category of 14
  pathologizing
    homosexuality 127
  pathology of 38
  psychoanalytic theory
    and practice 4, 11
Humanism 54
Humanistic modernism 4

Identification 3
  ego 70, 83
  melancholic 148

primary 53
representation 3–4
Identities continuous
  in time 105–113
Indolence 164–167
  conscience of 165
Insomnia, relentless
  vigilance of
  anonymous existence 162–164
  Levinas's
    phenomenological
    analyses of insomnia 163
Intersubjectivity 130
Intra-psychic dynamics 25

Jungian analytical trainings 158
Jung's theorizing of creativity 113

Kieran's
  fatigue 169–173
  lethargic reluctance 172
Kleinian, mission of meta-
  psychology 38
Kleinian psychoanalysis 35
  normativeness of 42
Klein, Melanie 35
  methods of investigation 41
  model 41
  Oedipus complex 37
  position on language 45
  pre-Oedipal, pre-linguistic,
    object relations 37
  theory of symbol formation 39
Kraft-Ebbing 14
Kristeva
  Desire in Language 51
  elaboration of psychoanalytical
    notions 57
  originality 51
  Powers of Horror 52
  Psychoanalysis
    and the Polis 49

Lacan
    mother-infant relationship 115
Lacanian psychoanalysis 118
Lesbian, 124–126
    acknowledgement
        of attachments 149
    butch-femme identifications 15
    identity 15
    organization 15
    socio-historical
        specificity of 12
    with feminism 15
Lesbianism 140
Lesbianism and Psychoanalysis 3, 126
Lesbianism theory 3, 11–12
Levinas's
    as "beyond being" 161
    between effort
        and fatigue 167–168
    consciousness and the
        unconscious 162, 168
    Existence and Existents 157
    experiences in
        consulting room 156–161
    face-to-face encounter 150
    metaphors of space
        and time 162
    model of the face-to face
        relationship 47
    notion of the relation 115
    phenomenological analyses
        of insomnia 163
    theories of reflection 158
    theorizing 117
    view of instant 116
Limentani 16
Little, Margaret 53
Lived time 96–97
Lorde, Audre 13
Luigi's
    homosexuality 150
    moustache 144

sexuality 146
Lurching 167

Male-female binary 75
Malinowski, Bronislaw 61
Masculinity 70–71, 73
Masturbation 32
Melancholia 147–149
Meltzer, Donald 38, 43
    The Psychoanalytical Process 44
Merleau-Ponty
    account of embodied
        subjectivity 83
    account of embodiment 78
    account of subjectivity 79
    concept of subjectivity 106
    critique of naturalism 79
    critique of the notion
        of body 131
    language and
        embodiment 130–131
    lived present 102–105
    notion of embodiment 78
    notion of identity 116
    notion of intentional
        embodied subject 79
    notions of sexuality 133
    phenomenological
        approach 129
    *Phenomenology
        of Perception* 77
    theorizing of temporality 105,
        107, 115
Meta-psychological nosology 39
Methodist community 88
Mitchell, Juliet, *The Selected
    Melanie Klein* 40
Modernism 2
Modernity
    enlightenment 2
    humanism 2
    Kant's philosophy 2–3

Mother-identification 71
Mother-infant relationship 115

Narcissism 52–54
National Socialism in Germany 99
National Socialism's stance 99
Negativism, symbolic
     integration of 49
Neuropsychiatry 39
Non-object-orientated layers 53

Object relations schools 59
O'Connor, Noreen 1, 11–12, 35, 47,
     85, 126, 136, 139, 146, 153
     feminist reading 116
Oedipus complex 12, 37, 51, 61, 70,
     72, 75, 90, 127, 135, 141
Oedipal interpretations
     femininity 2
     masculinity 2
     sexual desires 2
Oedipal negation 53
Onanism 37
Other's time 114–118

Perversion, subjects 85–93
Phobia, narcissism,
     borderline psychosis 52–54
Passionate differences 1–10
Paranoid schizoid position 1, 44
Phobias, groups of 140
     of situations 140
Post-modernism 2, 92
Post-modernists 4, 85
     model of communication 45
Potentiality-for-being 98
Power 2, 66–67
Psychoanalysis
     an-arche of 47–57
     contradictions with
          sexual difference 56
     cornerstone of 3

foundationalism and
     the search for origin 50–51
     personal 107
     self-referential nature of 44
     transforming 128–129
Psychoanalysts 6
     homosexuality 10
Psychoanalytic
     conceptualisation 40
     discourses 16
     practices,
          phenomenology 129–130
The Psycho-Analytic Play
     Technique 36
Psychoanalytic theorizing,
     "pre-oedipal" of 18
Psychoanalytic theory
     and practice 17, 43
Psychopathia Sexualis 14
Psychopathology, symptom of 32
Psychotherapeutic validators,
     ethical vigilance of 154
Psychotic bits 42

Racism 24
Really heterosexual 9
Really lesbian 10
Reasonable ego, mechanics
     of 61–64
Relentless vigilance of
     anonymous existence 162–164
Representation 3–4
Repressive hypothesis 4
Retention 103
Rosen, Ismond 16
Ryan, Joanna, Wild Desires
     and Mistaken Identities 3, 7,
     10–11, 126, 136, 139, 146
Ryan, Tom 111

Sackville-West, Vita 16
Sameness 10

Same-sex love 136
Same-sex sexuality 16, 80, 134
Segal, Hannah 16
    Kleinian theory
        and practice 39
Self-identical entity 4
    psychoanalysis 35
Self-possession 41
Sexual
    aberration 14
    disposition 72
    identity 4, 11
    orientation 15
    preference 15
Sexuality 5, 131–134, 145
    discourse of 43
    falsity of 44
    images of 121–137
    possibilities of 32
    questions of 122–124
Socio-cultural
    factors 25
    specificity 90
Spivak, Gayatri 33
Stabat mater 56
Subjectivity 61, 76
    between being
        and non-being 111
    temporality of 110
Sublimation 69
Super-ego 64–67, 70, 74, 77, 80
    embodied 77–84
    Freud's concept of 77
    scrutiny of 77
Symbolisation 38–39
Symbolism 37
Symptomatology 158

The Magic Mountain 96
The Second Sex 105
Three Essays on Sexuality 15
Thrownness 100, 102
Timeless absorption 113–114
Transference and
    counter-transference 123

Unconscious feelings
    and ideas 68
Unconsciousness 162, 168
Universalism 117
Unnameable 52–54
Unnatural sexuality 14
Utopia 91–93

Voices and sexualities 11

Washington Times Socarides 16
Watersports
    (sex with urination) 30
Weariness 164–167
Welsh Methodist family 86
Whisman Vera 15
Whitebook, Joel, modernist 85
*Wild Desires and
    Mistaken Identities* 3, 7, 10, 126
Wildness 30
Winnicott's theorizing
    of creativity 113
Wishing 98
Woolf, Virginia 16
Word-presentations 64

Young-Bruehl, *Anatomy
    of Prejudice* 141–142